The Latest Easy

Instant Pot

Cookbook for Beginners

1800+ Quick & Healthy Instant Pot Recipes for Busy Days, Step By Step for Cooking Simple and Wholesome Homemade Meals

Carol E. McPherson

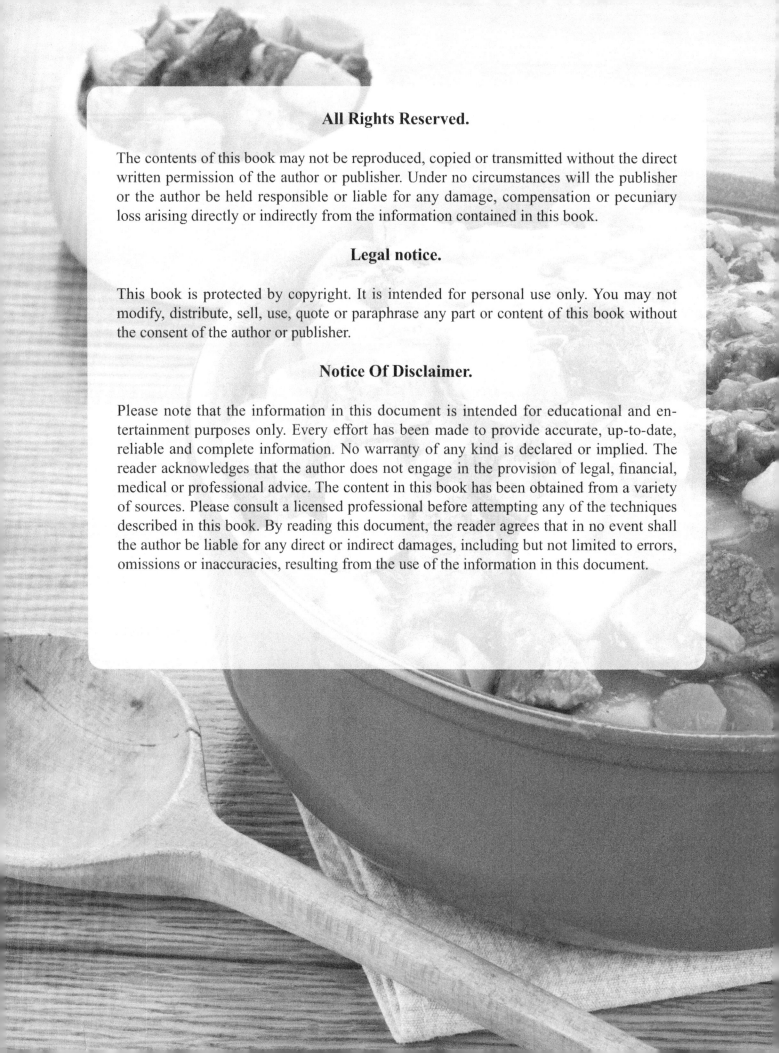

CONTENTS

INTRODUCTION

Carol E. McPherson is a culinary enthusiast, cookbook author, and a well-known figure in the world of pressure cooking. With years of experience in crafting delicious recipes for various culinary appliances, she has become a trusted name among home cooks and Instant Pot enthusiasts. Carol's passion for creating flavorful, convenient, and healthy meals has led her to explore the limitless possibilities of the Instant Pot. Her dedication to making cooking enjoyable and accessible is evident in her writing and culinary creations.

So, why the Instant Pot? It's not just another kitchen appliance; it's a game-changer. Its versatility, speed, and precision make it an indispensable tool for any cook. And with Carol's guidance, you'll harness its full potential, transforming ordinary ingredients into extraordinary meals in a fraction of the time it would take with conventional cooking methods.

As you delve into the pages of this cookbook, you'll discover a treasure trove of recipes that cover a wide spectrum of cuisines, tastes, and dietary preferences. From hearty stews that warm your soul on a chilly evening to quick and easy weekday dinners that save you time without sacrificing flavor, Carol's recipes are as diverse as they are delicious. Vegetarian, vegan, gluten-free, or simply in search of a comforting classic? You'll find options that cater to your specific needs and cravings. Whether you're a busy parent juggling work and family or an aspiring home chef eager to expand your repertoire, Carol's Instant Pot Cookbook empowers you to prepare restaurant-quality meals without the fuss.

WHY INSTANT POT?

The Instant Pot, often hailed as a kitchen game-changer, is a versatile and time-saving electric pressure cooker that has become a must-have appliance for countless households. Combining multiple kitchen appliances into one, it serves as a pressure cooker, slow cooker, rice cooker, sauté pan, steamer, and more, all in a single countertop device. With its ability to significantly speed up cooking times and its diverse cooking functions, the Instant Pot makes preparing a wide range of dishes, from hearty stews to tender roasts, quick and effortless. Its user-friendly interface and safety features, such as pressure release valves and automated settings, have made it an indispensable tool for busy home cooks seeking convenience without sacrificing flavor and nutrition.

Time Efficiency: It drastically reduces cooking times, making it perfect for busy individuals who want meals prepared quickly.

Nutrient Retention: Pressure cooking preserves the nutrients in food, resulting in healthier and more flavorful dishes.

Set-and-Forget: With programmable settings and automated functions, it allows users to start cooking and go about their day without constant monitoring.

Consistency: The Instant Pot consistently produces tender and evenly cooked meals, reducing the risk of overcooking or burning.

WHAT THE INSTANT POT CAN AND CAN'T DO

Do's

Use Proper Liquid Amount

Always include enough liquid (usually at least one cup) in your recipes to create steam and build pressure.

Layer Ingredients Appropriately

Layer ingredients in a way that prevents burning or sticking, with denser items at the bottom and liquids on top.

Seal the Lid Properly

Ensure the Instant Pot's sealing ring is in place, and the float valve moves freely before sealing the lid.

Follow Cooking Times

Adhere to recommended cooking times in recipes to achieve desired results.

Use the Right Release Method

Know when to use natural release (allowing pressure to drop naturally) and quick release (manually releasing pressure) based on the recipe.

Clean After Each Use

Clean the Instant Pot thoroughly after each use to prevent residual odors and maintain hygiene.

Don'ts

Overfill the Pot

Avoid overfilling the Instant Pot, especially when cooking foods that expand or release steam, to prevent clogs and pressure build-up.

Block the Steam Release Valve

Never block the steam release valve with your hand or other objects during operation.

Skip the Liquid

Always use the minimum required liquid specified in the recipe; insufficient liquid can lead to scorching and uneven cooking.

Open Under Pressure

Never force open the Instant Pot when it's pressurized; wait for the pressure to release naturally or use quick release if necessary.

Use It Unattended

While the Instant Pot is safe, it's essential not to leave it unattended during cooking, especially when using quick release.

Add Dairy Early

When cooking with dairy products (like milk or cream), add them after pressure cooking to prevent curdling.

Use Expired Sealing Rings

Check and replace the sealing ring if it's damaged or has exceeded its lifespan to maintain proper sealing and safety.

INSTANT POT CLEANING AND MAINTE-NANCE

1. Before cleaning, make sure the Instant Pot is unplugged and completely cooled to avoid accidents.

2. Remove the stainless steel inner pot from the bottom of the Instant Pot. Wash in dishwasher or by hand.

3. Remove the sealing ring, steam release valve and plug shield from the Instant Pot lid.

4. Inspect sealing ring for residue or odors. Wash in warm soapy water and make sure it is completely dry before putting it back in place.

5. Wipe down the exterior of the Instant Pot, including the control panel, with a damp cloth or sponge. Be careful not to allow water to penetrate the control area.

6. Remove the steam release valve and clean with warm, soapy water. Make sure there are no food particles or residue.

7. Inspect the float valve for any debris or buildup. Clean with a soft brush or cloth.

8. Clean the housing and heating elements with a dry or damp cloth (unplug the Instant Pot). Be careful not to let water drip into the base.

By following these step-by-step instructions, you can easily clean and care for your Instant Pot to ensure its longevity and continued reliable performance.

Breakfast

Breakfast

Savory Roast Beef Sandwiches

Servings: 8

Cooking Time: 1 Hour 30 Minutes

Ingredients:

- 2 ½ lb beef roast
- 2 tbsp olive oil
- 1 onion, chopped
- 4 garlic cloves, minced
- ½ cup dry red wine
- 2 cups beef broth stock
- 16 slices Fontina cheese
- 8 split hoagie rolls
- Salt and pepper to taste

Directions:

1. Season the beef with salt and pepper. Warm oil on Sauté and brown the beef for 2 to 3 minutes per side; reserve. Add onion and garlic to the pot and cook for 3 minutes until translucent. Set aside. Add red wine to deglaze. Mix in beef broth and take back the beef. Seal the lid and cook on High Pressure for 50 minutes. Release the pressure naturally for 10 minutes. Preheat a broiler.
2. Transfer the beef to a cutting board and slice. Roll the meat and top with onion. Each sandwich should be topped with 2 Fontina cheese slices. Place the sandwiches under the broiler for 2-3 minutes until the cheese melts.

Strawberry Jam

Servings: 6

Cooking Time: 30 Minutes

Ingredients:

- 1 lb strawberries, chopped
- 1 cup sugar
- ½ lemon, juiced and zested
- 1 tbsp mint, chopped

Directions:

1. Add the strawberries, sugar, lemon juice, and zest to the Instant Pot. Seal the lid, select manual, and cook for 2 minutes on High.
2. Release pressure naturally for 10 minutes. Open the lid and stir in chopped mint. Select Sauté and continue cooking until the jam thickens, about 10 minutes. Let to cool before serving.

Brunchy Sausage Bowl

Servings:4

Cooking Time: 10 Minutes

Ingredients:

- 1 pound pork sausage links
- 2 large potatoes, peeled and thinly sliced
- 1 medium red bell pepper, seeded and diced
- 1 medium sweet onion, peeled and diced
- 1 can creamed corn
- ½ teaspoon sea salt
- ¼ teaspoon ground black pepper
- ¾ cup tomato juice

Directions:

1. Press the Sauté button on Instant Pot. Add sausage links and brown for 4–5 minutes. Move the sausages to a plate.
2. Layer the potatoes, bell pepper, onion, and corn in the Instant Pot. Sprinkle with salt and pepper. Place sausage links on top of the corn. Pour the tomato juice over the top of the other ingredients in the Instant Pot. Lock lid.
3. Press the Manual button and adjust time to 5 minutes. When the timer beeps, let the pressure release naturally for at least 10 minutes.
4. Quick-release any additional pressure until the float valve drops and then unlock lid. Serve warm.

Sweet Potato Morning Hash

Servings:4

Cooking Time: 10 Minutes

Ingredients:

- 6 large eggs
- 1 tablespoon Italian seasoning
- ½ teaspoon sea salt
- ½ teaspoon ground black pepper
- ½ pound ground pork sausage
- 1 large sweet potato, peeled and cubed
- 1 small onion, peeled and diced
- 2 cloves garlic, minced
- 1 medium green bell pepper, seeded and diced
- 2 cups water

Directions:

1. In a medium bowl, whisk together eggs, Italian seasoning, salt, and pepper. Set aside.
2. Press the Sauté button on Instant Pot. Stir-fry sausage, sweet potato, onion, garlic, and bell pepper for 3–5 minutes until onions are translucent.
3. Transfer mixture to a 7-cup greased glass dish. Pour whisked eggs over the sausage mixture.
4. Place trivet in Instant Pot. Pour in water. Place dish with egg mixture onto trivet. Lock lid.
5. Press the Manual button and adjust time to 5 minutes. When timer beeps, quick-release pressure until float valve drops and then unlock lid. Remove dish from Instant Pot. Let sit at room temperature for 5–10 minutes to allow the eggs to set. Slice and serve.

French Cheese & Spinach Quiche

Servings: 5

Cooking Time: 20 Minutes

Ingredients:

- 1 lb spinach, chopped
- ½ cup mascarpone cheese
- ½ cup feta cheese, shredded
- 3 eggs, beaten
- ½ cup goat cheese
- 3 tbsp butter
- ½ cup milk
- 1 pack pie dough

Directions:

1. In a bowl, mix spinach, eggs, mascarpone, feta and goat cheeses. Dust a clean surface with flour and unfold the pie sheets onto it. Using a rolling pin, roll the dough to fit your Instant Pot. Repeat with the other sheets. Combine milk and butter in a skillet. Bring to a boil and melt the butter completely. Remove from the heat.
2. Grease a baking pan with oil. Place in 2 pie sheets and brush with milk mixture. Make the first layer of spinach mixture and cover with another two pie sheets. Again, brush with butter and milk mixture, and repeat until you have used all ingredients. Pour 1 cup water into your Instant Pot and insert a trivet. Lower the pan on the trivet. Seal the lid. Cook on High Pressure for 6 minutes. Do a quick release. Place parchment paper under the pie to use it as a lifting method to remove the pie. Serve cold.

Italian Egg Cakes

Servings: 4

Cooking Time: 25 Minutes

Ingredients:

- ¼ cup ricotta cheese, cubed
- ½ cup mozzarella, shredded
- 1 cup chopped baby spinach
- 6 beaten eggs
- 1 chopped tomato
- Salt and pepper to taste
- 2 tbsp basil, chopped

Directions:

1. Pour 1 cup of water into the Instant Pot and fit in a trivet. Place spinach in small cups. Combine eggs, mozzarella cheese, ricotta cheese, tomato, salt, and pepper in a bowl. Fill 3/4 of each cup with the mixture and top with basil.
2. Place the cups on top of the trivet and seal the lid. Select Manual and cook for 15 minutes on High pressure. Once ready, perform a quick pressure release. Serve hot.

Crustless Crab Quiche

Servings:6

Cooking Time: 10 Minutes

Ingredients:

- 6 large eggs
- ¼ cup unsweetened almond milk
- 2 teaspoons fresh thyme leaves
- ½ teaspoon sea salt
- ¼ teaspoon ground black pepper
- ½ teaspoon hot sauce
- ½ pound crabmeat
- ¼ cup crumbled goat cheese
- 2 thick slices bacon, diced
- ¼ cup peeled and diced onion
- ¼ cup seeded and diced green bell pepper
- 2 cups water

Directions:

1. In a medium bowl, whisk eggs, milk, thyme leaves, salt, pepper, and hot sauce. Stir in crabmeat and goat cheese. Set aside.
2. Grease a 7-cup glass dish. Set aside.
3. Press the Sauté button on Instant Pot. Add diced bacon and brown for 2 minutes, rendering some fat. Add onion and bell pepper and stir-fry with bacon until tender. Transfer mixture to the glass container. Pour in egg mixture.
4. Place trivet in Instant Pot. Pour in water. Place dish with egg mixture onto trivet. Lock lid.
5. Press the Manual button and adjust time to 5 minutes. When timer beeps, let pressure release naturally for 10 minutes. Quick-release any additional pressure until float valve drops and then unlock lid.
6. Remove dish from Instant Pot. Let cool for 10 minutes to allow eggs to set. Slice and serve.

Western Omelet Casserole

Servings:4

Cooking Time: 10 Minutes

Ingredients:

- 6 large eggs

- ½ teaspoon sea salt
- ½ teaspoon ground black pepper
- 2 dashes hot sauce
- 1 cup diced ham
- 1 small red bell pepper, seeded and diced
- 1 small green bell pepper, seeded and diced
- 1 small onion, peeled and diced
- 2 cups water

Directions:

1. In a medium bowl, whisk together eggs, salt, pepper, and hot sauce. Set aside.
2. Press the Sauté button on Instant Pot. Stir-fry ham, bell peppers, and onion for 3–5 minutes or until onions are translucent.
3. Transfer mixture to a greased 7-cup glass dish. Pour whisked eggs over the ham mixture.
4. Place trivet in Instant Pot. Pour in water. Place dish with egg mixture onto trivet. Lock lid.
5. Press the Manual button and adjust time to 5 minutes. When timer beeps, quick-release pressure until float valve drops and then unlock lid.
6. Remove dish from the Instant Pot. Let sit at room temperature for 5–10 minutes to allow the eggs to set. Slice and serve.

Speedy Soft-boiled Eggs

Servings: 4

Cooking Time: 10 Minutes

Ingredients:

- 4 large eggs
- Salt and pepper to taste

Directions:

1. To the pressure cooker, add 1 cup of water and place a wire rack. Place eggs on it. Seal the lid, press Steam, and cook for 3 minutes on High Pressure. Do a quick release.
2. Allow to cool in an ice bath. Peel the eggs and season with salt and pepper before serving.

Breakfast Frittata

Servings: 4

Cooking Time: 25 Minutes

Ingredients:

- 8 beaten eggs
- 1 cup cherry tomatoes, halved
- 1 tbsp Dijon mustard
- 1 cup mushrooms, chopped
- Salt and pepper to taste
- 1 cup sharp cheddar, grated

Directions:

1. Combine the eggs, mushrooms, mustard, salt, pepper, and ½ cup of cheddar cheese in a bowl. Pour in a greased baking pan and top with the remaining cheddar cheese and cherry tomatoes. Add 1 cup of water to your Instant Pot and fit in a trivet. Place the baking pan on the trivet.
2. Seal the lid. Select Manual and cook for 15 minutes on High. When ready, perform a quick pressure release and unlock the lid. Slice into wedges before serving.

Egg Muffins To Go

Servings: 3

Cooking Time: 15 Minutes

Ingredients:

- 1 tablespoon olive oil
- 3 pieces bacon, diced
- 1 small onion, peeled and diced
- 4 large eggs
- 2 teaspoons Italian seasoning
- ½ teaspoon sea salt
- ½ teaspoon ground black pepper
- ¼ cup shredded Cheddar cheese
- 1 small Roma tomato, diced
- ¼ cup chopped spinach
- 1 cup water

Directions:

1. Press the Sauté button on Instant Pot. Heat olive oil. Add bacon and onion and stir-fry 3–5 minutes until onions are translucent. Transfer mixture to a small bowl to cool.
2. In a medium bowl, whisk together eggs, Italian seasoning, salt, black pepper, cheese, tomatoes, and spinach. Stir in cooled bacon mixture.
3. Place trivet into Instant Pot. Pour in water. Place steamer basket on trivet.
4. Distribute egg mixture evenly among 6 silicone muffin cups. Carefully place cups on steamer basket. Lock lid.
5. Press the Manual button and adjust time to 8 minutes. When the timer beeps, quick-release pressure until float valve drops and then unlock lid.
6. Remove egg muffins and serve warm.

Cinnamon Roll Doughnut Holes

Servings: 14

Cooking Time: 16 Minutes

Ingredients:

- 1 package Krusteaz Cinnamon Roll Supreme Mix (includes icing packet)
- 6 tablespoons unsalted butter, melted
- ½ cup cold water
- ¼ cup chopped pecans
- 1 cup water

Directions:

1. In a medium bowl, combine dry mix, butter, and ½ cup cold water. Fold in pecans. Spoon half of batter into a greased seven-hole silicone egg mold. If your egg mold has a silicone top, use this. If your egg mold came with a plastic top, do not use. Instead, cover with aluminum foil.
2. Add 1 cup water to the Instant Pot and insert steam rack. Place egg mold on steam rack. Lock lid.
3. Press the Manual or Pressure Cook button and adjust time to 8 minutes. When timer beeps, quick-release pressure until float valve drops. Unlock lid.
4. Pop doughnut holes out of egg mold and repeat with remaining batter.
5. When doughnut holes are cooled, mix icing packet with 1 ½ tablespoons water and dip doughnut holes into glaze to cover. Serve.

Blueberry-oat Muffins

Servings: 6

Cooking Time: 9 Minutes

Ingredients:

- 1 cup all-purpose baking flour
- ¼ cup old-fashioned oats
- 2 teaspoons baking powder
- ½ teaspoon baking soda
- ⅛ teaspoon salt
- ½ teaspoon vanilla extract
- 3 tablespoons unsalted butter, melted
- 2 large eggs
- 4 tablespoons granulated sugar
- ⅓ cup blueberries
- 1 cup water

Directions:

1. Grease six silicone cupcake liners.
2. In a large bowl, combine flour, oats, baking powder, baking soda, and salt.
3. In a medium bowl, combine vanilla, butter, eggs, and sugar.
4. Pour wet ingredients from medium bowl into the bowl with dry ingredients. Gently combine ingredients. Do not overmix. Fold in blueberries, then spoon mixture into prepared cupcake liners.
5. Add water to the Instant Pot and insert steam rack. Place cupcake liners on top. Lock lid.
6. Press the Manual or Pressure Cook button and adjust time to 9 minutes. When timer beeps, quick-release pressure until float valve drops. Unlock lid.
7. Remove muffins from pot and set aside to cool 30 minutes. Serve.

Greek Yogurt With Honey & Walnuts

Servings: 10

Cooking Time: 15hr

Ingredients:

- 2 tbsp Greek yogurt
- 8 cups milk
- ¼ cup sugar honey
- 1 tsp vanilla extract
- 1 cup walnuts, chopped

Directions:

1. Add the milk to your Instant Pot. Seal the lid and press Yogurt until the display shows "Boil". When the cooking cycle is over, the display will show Yogurt. Open the lid and check that milk temperature is at least 175°F. Get rid of the skin lying on the milk's surface. Let cool in an ice bath until it becomes warm to the touch.
2. In a bowl, mix one cup of milk and yogurt to make a smooth consistency. Mix the milk with yogurt mixture. Transfer to the pot and place on your Pressure cooker.
3. Seal the lid, press Yogurt, and adjust the timer to 9 hrs. Once cooking is complete, strain the yogurt into a bowl using a strainer with cheesecloth. Chill for 4 hours.
4. Add in vanilla and honey and gently stir well. Spoon the yogurt into glass jars. Serve sprinkled with walnuts and enjoy.

Tofu Hash Brown Breakfast

Servings: 4

Cooking Time: 21 Minutes

Ingredients:

- 1 cup tofu cubes
- 2 cups frozen hash browns
- 8 beaten eggs
- 1 cup shredded cheddar
- ¼ cup milk
- Salt and pepper to taste

Directions:

1. Set your Instant Pot to Sauté. Place in tofu and cook until browned on all sides, about 4 minutes. Add in hash brown and cook for 2 minutes. Beat eggs, cheddar cheese, milk, salt, and pepper in a bowl and pour over hash brown. Seal the lid, select Manual, and cook for 5 minutes on High. Once done, perform a quick pressure release. Cut into slices before serving.

Pimiento Cheese Grits

Servings: 4

Cooking Time: 10 Minutes

Ingredients:

- ¾ cup plus 1 ½ cups water, divided
- 1 cup stone-ground grits
- 2 tablespoons unsalted butter
- 1 teaspoon salt
- ½ teaspoon ground black pepper
- ½ cup grated sharp Cheddar cheese
- 1 jar diced pimientos, drained

Directions:

1. Add ¾ cup water to the Instant Pot and insert steam rack.
2. In a 7-cup glass baking dish that fits down into the pot insert, combine grits, butter, remaining 1 ½ cups water, salt, and pepper. Lock lid.
3. Press the Rice button. When timer beeps, quick-release pressure until float valve drops. Unlock lid.
4. Stir in cheese and pimientos. Serve warm.

Chicken Sandwiches With Barbecue Sauce

Servings: 4

Cooking Time: 50 Minutes

Ingredients:

- 4 chicken thighs, boneless and skinless
- 2 cups barbecue sauce
- 1 onion, minced
- 2 garlic cloves, minced
- 2 tbsp minced fresh parsley
- 1 tbsp lemon juice
- 1 tbsp mayonnaise
- 2 cups lettuce, shredded
- 4 burger buns

Directions:

1. Into the pot, place the garlic, onion, and barbecue sauce. Add in the chicken and toss it to coat. Seal the lid and cook on High Pressure for 15 minutes. Do a natural release for 10 minutes. Use two forks to shred the chicken and mix it into the sauce. Press Keep Warm and let the mixture simmer for 15 minutes to thicken the sauce until the desired consistency.
2. In a bowl, mix lemon juice, mayonnaise, and parsley; toss lettuce into the mixture to coat. Separate the chicken into equal parts to match the burger buns; top with lettuce and complete the sandwiches.

Tomato Mozzarella Basil Egg Bites

Servings: 6

Cooking Time: 8 Minutes

Ingredients:

- 4 large eggs
- 2 tablespoons grated yellow onion
- ½ teaspoon salt
- ½ teaspoon ground black pepper
- 6 cherry tomatoes, quartered
- ¼ cup grated mozzarella cheese
- 2 tablespoons chopped fresh basil
- 1 cup water

Directions:

1. Grease six silicone cupcake liners.
2. In a medium bowl, whisk together eggs, onion, salt, and pepper. Distribute egg mixture evenly among cupcake liners. Add tomatoes, cheese, and basil to each cup.
3. Add water to the Instant Pot and insert steam rack. Place steamer basket on steam rack. Carefully place cupcake liners in basket. Lock lid.
4. Press the Manual or Pressure Cook button and adjust time to 8 minutes. When timer beeps, quick-release pressure until float valve drops. Unlock lid.
5. Remove egg bites. Serve warm.

Grandma's Country Gravy

Servings: 6

Cooking Time: 16 Minutes

Ingredients:

- 2 tablespoons unsalted butter
- 1 pound ground pork sausage
- 1 small sweet onion, peeled and diced
- ¼ cup chicken broth
- ¼ cup all-purpose flour
- 1 ½ cups heavy cream
- ½ teaspoon salt
- 1 tablespoon ground black pepper

Directions:

1. Press the Sauté button on the Instant Pot. Add butter and heat until melted. Add sausage and onion and stir-fry 3–5 minutes until onions are translucent. The pork will still be a little pink in places. Add broth. Press the Cancel button. Lock lid.
2. Press the Manual or Pressure Cook button and adjust time to 1 minute. When timer beeps, quick-release pressure until float valve drops. Unlock lid. Whisk in flour, cream, salt, and pepper.
3. Press the Keep Warm button and let the gravy sit about 5–10 minutes to allow to thicken. Remove from heat. Serve warm.

Pumpkin Spice Latte French Toast Casserole

Servings:4

Cooking Time: 20 Minutes

Ingredients:

- 4 cups cubed whole-wheat bread
- 1½ cups whole milk
- ¼ cup brewed coffee, cooled
- 3 large eggs
- ¼ cup pumpkin purée
- 1 teaspoon vanilla extract
- ¼ cup pure maple syrup
- 2 teaspoons pumpkin pie spice
- Pinch of sea salt
- 3 tablespoons butter, cut into 3 pats
- 1 cup water

Directions:

1. Grease a 7-cup glass dish. Add bread. Set aside.
2. In a medium bowl, whisk together milk, coffee, eggs, pumpkin purée, vanilla, maple syrup, pumpkin pie spice, and salt. Pour over bread; place pats of butter on top.
3. Pour water into Instant Pot. Set trivet in Instant Pot. Place glass dish on top of trivet. Lock lid.
4. Press the Manual button and adjust time to 20 minutes. When the timer beeps, quick-release the pressure until float valve drops and then unlock lid.
5. Remove glass bowl from the Instant Pot. Transfer to a rack until cool. Serve.

Sunday Brunch Sausage Gravy

Servings:10

Cooking Time: 10 Minutes

Ingredients:

- 2 tablespoons butter
- 1 pound ground pork sausage
- 1 small sweet onion, peeled and diced
- ¼ cup chicken broth
- ¼ cup all-purpose flour
- 1½ cups heavy cream
- ½ teaspoon sea salt
- 1 tablespoon ground black pepper

Directions:

1. Press the Sauté button on the Instant Pot. Add butter and heat until melted. Add pork sausage and onion. Stir-fry 3–5 minutes until onions are translucent. The pork will still be a little pink in places. Add chicken broth. Lock lid.
2. Press the Manual button and adjust time to 1 minute. When the timer beeps, quick-release the pressure until the float valve drops and then unlock the lid. Whisk in flour, cream, salt, and pepper.
3. Press the Keep Warm button and let the gravy sit for about 5–10 minutes to allow the sauce to thicken. Remove from heat and serve warm.

Light & Fruity Yogurt

Servings: 12

Cooking Time: 24hr

Ingredients:

- ¼ cup Greek yogurt containing active cultures
- 1 lb raspberries, mashed
- 1 cup sugar
- 3 tbsp gelatin
- 1 tbsp fresh orange juice
- 8 cups milk

Directions:

1. In a bowl, add sugar and raspberries and stir well to dissolve the sugar. Let sit for 30 minutes at room temperature. Add in orange juice and gelatin and mix well until dissolved. Remove the mixture and place in a sealable container, close, and allow to sit for 12 hrs to 24 hrs at room temperature before placing in the fridge. Refrigerate for a maximum of 2 weeks.
2. Into the cooker, add milk, and close the lid. The steam vent should be set to Venting then to Sealing. Select Yogurt until "Boil" is showed on display. When complete, there will be a display of "Yogurt" on the screen.
3. Open the lid and using a food thermometer, ensure the milk temperature is at least 185°F. Transfer the steel pot to a wire rack and allow to cool for 30 minutes until the milk has reached 110°F.
4. In a bowl, mix ½ cup warm milk and yogurt. Transfer the mixture into the remaining warm milk and stir without having to scrape the steel pot's bottom. Take the steel pot back to the base of the pot and seal the lid.
5. Select Yogurt and cook for 8 hrs. Allow the yogurt to chill in a refrigerator for 1-2 hrs. Transfer the chilled yogurt to a bowl and stir in fresh raspberry jam.

Strawberry Cream-filled French Toast Casserole

Servings: 4

Cooking Time: 20 Minutes

Ingredients:

- 8 ounces cream cheese, room temperature
- ¼ cup sugar
- 2 cups sliced strawberries
- 1 tablespoon orange zest
- 4 cups cubed bread, dried out overnight, divided
- 2 cups whole milk
- 3 large eggs
- 1 teaspoon vanilla extract
- ¼ cup pure maple syrup
- Pinch of ground nutmeg
- Pinch of sea salt
- 3 tablespoons butter, cut into 3 pats
- 1 cup water
- 4 teaspoons powdered sugar

Directions:

1. In a large bowl, cream together the cream cheese and sugar by mashing ingredients with the tines of a fork. Fold in strawberries and orange zest. Set aside.
2. Grease a 7-cup glass dish. Add 2 cups bread. Spoon in a layer of the strawberry mixture. Add remaining 2 cups bread. Set aside.
3. In a medium bowl, whisk together milk, eggs, vanilla, maple syrup, nutmeg, and salt. Pour over bread; place pats of butter on top.
4. Pour water into Instant Pot. Set trivet in Instant Pot. Place glass dish on top of trivet. Lock lid.
5. Press the Manual button and adjust time to 20 minutes. When the timer beeps, quick-release pressure until float valve drops and then unlock lid.
6. Remove glass bowl from the Instant Pot. Transfer to a rack until cooled. Sprinkle with powdered sugar.

Southern Cheesy Grits

Servings:4

Cooking Time: 10 Minutes

Ingredients:

- ¾ plus 1½ cups water, divided
- 1 cup stone-ground grits
- 2 tablespoons butter
- 1 teaspoon sea salt
- ½ teaspoon ground black pepper
- ½ cup grated sharp Cheddar cheese

Directions:

1. Place ¾ cup water in the bottom of the Instant Pot. Insert the trivet.
2. In the stainless-steel bowl that fits down into the pot insert, stir together the grits, butter, remaining 1½ cups water, salt, and pepper. Lock lid.
3. Press the Rice button. When timer beeps, quick-release the pressure until the float valve drops and then unlock the lid. Stir in the cheese and serve warm.

Sausage And Sweet Potato Hash

Servings:4

Cooking Time: 10 Minutes

Ingredients:

- ½ pound ground pork sausage
- 1 large sweet potato, peeled and grated
- 1 small yellow onion, peeled and diced
- 2 cloves garlic, peeled and minced
- 1 medium green bell pepper, seeded and diced
- 1 tablespoon Italian seasoning
- ½ teaspoon salt
- ½ teaspoon ground black pepper
- 2 cups water

Directions:

1. Press the Sauté button on the Instant Pot. Stir-fry sausage, sweet potato, onion, garlic, bell pepper, Italian seasoning, salt, and black pepper 3–5 minutes until onions are translucent. Press the Cancel button.
2. Transfer mixture to a greased 7-cup glass baking dish.
3. Add water to the Instant Pot and insert steam rack. Place dish on steam rack. Lock lid.
4. Press the Manual or Pressure Cook button and adjust time to 5 minutes. When timer beeps, quick-release pressure until float valve drops. Unlock lid.
5. Remove dish from the Instant Pot. Spoon hash onto plates and serve.

Crustless Power Quiche

Servings:2

Cooking Time: 9 Minutes

Ingredients:

- 6 large eggs
- ½ teaspoon salt
- ½ teaspoon ground black pepper
- 2 teaspoons olive oil
- ½ cup diced red onion
- 1 medium red bell pepper, seeded and diced
- ¼ pound ground pork sausage
- 1 ½ cups water
- 1 medium avocado, peeled, pitted, and diced

Directions:

1. In a medium bowl, whisk together eggs, salt, and black pepper. Set aside.
2. Press the Sauté button on the Instant Pot and heat oil. Stir-fry onion, bell pepper, and sausage 3–4 minutes until sausage starts to brown and onions are tender. Press the Cancel button.
3. Transfer sausage mixture to a greased 7-cup glass bowl. Pour whisked eggs over the mixture.
4. Add water to the Instant Pot and insert steam rack. Place bowl with egg mixture on steam rack. Lock lid.
5. Press the Manual or Pressure Cook button and adjust time to 5 minutes. When timer beeps, quick-release pressure until float valve drops. Unlock lid.
6. Remove bowl from pot. Let sit at room temperature 5–10 minutes to allow the eggs to set, then remove quiche from bowl, slice, and garnish with avocado. Serve warm.

Tex-mex Breakfast

Servings: 4

Cooking Time: 10 Minutes

Ingredients:

- 6 large eggs
- ½ teaspoon sea salt
- ¼ teaspoon ground black pepper
- ⅛ teaspoon chili powder
- ½ cup shredded Cheddar cheese
- 1 small Roma tomato, diced
- 2 tablespoons butter
- 2 small Yukon gold potatoes, grated
- 2 cups cubed cooked ham
- 1 small onion, peeled and diced
- 1 small jalapeño, seeded and diced
- ½ cup sliced button mushrooms
- 2 cups water

Directions:

1. In a medium bowl, whisk together eggs, salt, pepper, and chili powder. Stir in cheese and tomato. Set aside.
2. Press the Sauté button on Instant Pot. Heat the butter and stir-fry potatoes, ham, onion, jalapeño, and mushrooms for approximately 5 minutes until the potatoes are tender and onions are translucent.
3. Transfer cooked mixture to a 7-cup greased glass dish. Pour whisked eggs over the potato mixture.
4. Place trivet in Instant Pot. Pour in water. Place dish with egg mixture onto trivet. Lock lid.
5. Press the Manual button and adjust time to 5 minutes. When timer beeps, quick-release pressure until float valve drops and then unlock lid.
6. Remove dish from the Instant Pot. Let sit at room temperature for 5–10 minutes to allow the eggs to set. Slice and serve warm.

Pumpkin Steel Cut Oats With Cinnamon

Servings: 4

Cooking Time: 25 Minutes

Ingredients:

- 1 tbsp butter
- 2 cups steel-cut oats
- ¼ tsp cinnamon
- 1 cup pumpkin puree
- 3 tbsp maple syrup
- 2 tsp pumpkin seeds, toasted

Directions:

1. Melt butter on Sauté. Add in cinnamon, oats, pumpkin puree, and 3 cups of water. Seal the lid, select Porridge and cook for 10 minutes on High Pressure to get a few bite oats or for 14 minutes to form soft oats. Do a quick release. Open the lid and stir in maple syrup. Top with pumpkin seeds and serve.

Bacon-poblano Morning Taters

Servings: 4

Cooking Time: 10 Minutes

Ingredients:

- 1 tablespoon olive oil
- 2 slices bacon, diced
- 1 small onion, peeled and diced
- 2 small poblano peppers, seeded and diced
- 4 cups small-diced russet potatoes
- 2 tablespoons ghee
- 2–3 cloves garlic, minced
- 1 teaspoon sea salt
- ½ teaspoon ground black pepper
- ½ cup water

Directions:

1. Press Sauté button on Instant Pot and heat oil. Add bacon, onion, and peppers. Stir-fry until onions are translucent, 3–5 minutes. Transfer mixture to a 7-cup glass dish. Toss in potatoes, ghee, garlic, salt, and pepper.
2. Insert trivet into Instant Pot. Pour in water. Place dish on trivet. Lock lid.
3. Press the Manual button and adjust time to 5 minutes. When the timer beeps, let the pressure release naturally until the float valve drops. Remove dish from pot and serve.

Lazy Steel Cut Oats With Coconut

Servings: 2

Cooking Time: 25 Minutes

Ingredients:

- 1 tsp coconut oil
- 1 cup steel-cut oats
- ¾ cup coconut milk
- ¼ cup sugar
- ½ tsp vanilla extract
- 1 tbsp shredded coconut

Directions:

1. Warm coconut oil on Sauté in your Instant Pot. Add oats and cook as you stir until soft and toasted. Add in milk, sugar, vanilla, and 2 cups water and stir. Seal the lid and press Porridge. Cook for 12 minutes on High Pressure. Set steam vent to Venting to release the pressure quickly. Open the lid. Add oats as you stir to mix any extra liquid. Top with coconut and serve.

Ham And Swiss Muffin Frittatas

Servings:3

Cooking Time: 15 Minutes

Ingredients:

- 1 tablespoon olive oil
- ¼ cup small-diced ham
- ¼ cup diced red bell pepper, seeded
- 4 large eggs
- ½ teaspoon sea salt
- ½ teaspoon ground black pepper
- ¼ cup shredded Swiss cheese
- 1 cup water

Directions:

1. Press the Sauté button on Instant Pot. Heat olive oil. Add ham and bell pepper and stir-fry 3–5 minutes until peppers are tender. Transfer mixture to a small bowl to cool.
2. In a medium bowl, whisk together eggs, salt, pep-

per, and Swiss cheese. Stir in cooled ham mixture.
3. Place trivet into Instant Pot. Pour in water. Place steamer basket on trivet.
4. Distribute egg mixture evenly among 6 silicone muffin cups. Carefully place cups on steamer basket. Lock lid.
5. Press the Manual button and adjust time to 8 minutes. When timer beeps, quick-release pressure until float valve drops and then unlock lid.
6. Remove frittatas and serve warm.

Georgia Peach French Toast Casserole

Servings:4

Cooking Time: 20 Minutes

Ingredients:

- 4 cups cubed French bread, dried out overnight
- 2 cups diced, peeled ripe peaches
- 1 cup whole milk
- 3 large eggs
- 1 teaspoon vanilla extract
- ¼ cup granulated sugar
- ⅛ teaspoon salt
- 3 tablespoons unsalted butter, cut into 3 pats
- 1 cup water

Directions:

1. Grease a 7-cup glass baking dish. Add bread to dish in an even layer. Add peaches in an even layer over bread. Set aside.
2. In a medium bowl, whisk together milk, eggs, vanilla, sugar, and salt. Pour over bread; place butter pats on top.
3. Add water to the Instant Pot and insert steam rack. Place glass baking dish on top of steam rack. Lock lid.
4. Press the Manual or Pressure Cook button and adjust time to 20 minutes. When timer beeps, quick-release pressure until float valve drops. Unlock lid.
5. Remove bowl and transfer to a cooling rack until set, about 20 minutes. Serve.

Appetizers, Soups & Sides

Appetizers, Soups & Sides

Chili Goose Stew

Servings: 6

Cooking Time: 20 Minutes

Ingredients:

- 1 onion, chopped
- 1 cup chicken broth
- 1 lb goose breasts
- 3 tbsp tamari sauce
- 1 tbsp sweetener
- 3 tbsp chili sauce
- Salt and pepper to taste
- ½ cup water

Directions:

1. Sprinkle goose breasts with salt and pepper. Place them in your Instant Pot. Mix the chicken broth, tamari sauce, sweetener, onion, chili sauce, salt. pepper, and water in a bowl and pour it over the goose. Seal the lid, select Manual, and cook for 15 minutes on High. Perform a quick pressure release. Serve topped with sauce.

Chicken Wings With Teriyaki Sauce

Servings: 6

Cooking Time: 25 Minutes

Ingredients:

- 1 tbsp honey
- 1 cup teriyaki sauce
- 1 tsp black pepper
- 2 lb chicken wings
- 2 tbsp cornstarch
- 1 tsp sesame seeds

Directions:

1. In the pot, combine honey, teriyaki sauce, and black pepper until the honey dissolves. Toss in chicken wings to coat. Seal the lid, press Manual, and cook for 10 minutes on High. Release the pressure quickly. Transfer chicken wings to a platter. Mix 2 tbsp of water with the cornstarch. Press Sauté and stir the slurry into the sauce. Cook for 4 minutes until thickened. Top the chicken wings with the thickened sauce. Add a garnish of sesame seeds and serve.

Mediterranean Soup With Tortellini

Servings: 4

Cooking Time: 40 Minutes

Ingredients:

- 1 cup cream of mushroom soup
- ½ cup mushrooms, chopped
- 9 oz refrigerated tortellini
- 1 cup green peas
- 2 carrots, chopped
- 2 tbsp olive oil
- 2 shallots, chopped
- 2 garlic cloves, minced
- ½ tsp oregano
- 3 cups vegetable broth
- Salt and pepper to taste
- 2 tbsp Parmesan, shredded

Directions:

1. Heat the olive oil in your Instant Pot on Sauté. Add in shallots and garlic and cook for 3 minutes until translucent. Add in the carrots and mushrooms and continue sautéing for 3-4 minutes. Pour in broth, mushroom soup, and oregano, and tomatoes and seal the lid. Select Manual and cook for 7 minutes on High.
2. Once over, allow a natural release for 10 minutes, then perform a quick pressure release and unlock the lid. Stir in green peas and tortellini and cook for 3-5 minutes on Sauté. Sprinkle with Parmesan cheese and serve.

Mediterranean Carrot & Chickpea Soup

Servings: 6

Cooking Time: 15 Minutes

Ingredients:

- 14 oz can chickpeas
- 2 carrots, chopped
- 2 onions, chopped
- 2 tomatoes, chopped
- 3 tbsp tomato paste
- 2 tbsp chopped parsley
- 2 cups vegetable broth
- 2 tbsp olive oil
- 1 tsp salt

Directions:

1. Add in chickpeas, oil, onions, carrots, and tomatoes. Pour in the broth and sprinkle salt. Stir in the paste and seal the lid. Cook on High Pressure for 6 minutes. Do a quick release. Carefully unlock the lid. Remove the meal to a serving place. Sprinkle with parsley and serve.

Spicy Ground Beef Soup

Servings: 4

Cooking Time: 30 Minutes

Ingredients:

- 2 tbsp butter
- 3 oz cream cheese
- 7-oz ground beef
- 4 cups beef broth
- 2 garlic cloves, minced
- 1 tsp chili powder
- 1 tsp ground cumin
- ½ cup heavy cream
- Salt and pepper to taste

Directions:

1. Melt butter in your Instant Pot on Sauté. Place the ground beef and cook for 5-7 minutes and strain excess fat. Add in cream cheese, garlic, chili powder, ground cumin, heavy cream, salt, black pepper, and beef broth.
2. Seal the lid, select Pressure Cook, and cook for 5 minutes on High pressure. When done, allow a natural release for 10 minutes and unlock the lid. Serve warm.

Hearty Minestrone Soup

Servings:4

Cooking Time: 30 Minutes

Ingredients:

- 2 cups dried Great Northern beans
- 1 cup orzo
- 2 large carrots, peeled and diced
- 1 bunch Swiss chard, ribs removed and roughly chopped
- 1 medium zucchini, diced
- 2 stalks celery, diced
- 1 medium onion, peeled and diced
- 1 teaspoon minced garlic
- 1 tablespoon Italian seasoning
- 1 teaspoon salt
- ½ teaspoon ground black pepper
- 2 bay leaves
- 1 can diced tomatoes, including juice
- 4 cups vegetable broth
- 1 cup tomato juice
- 4 sprigs fresh parsley for garnish

Directions:

1. Rinse beans and add to the Instant Pot with remaining ingredients except parsley. Lock the lid.
2. Press the Soup button and cook for the default time of 30 minutes. When timer beeps, let pressure release naturally for 10 minutes.
3. Quick-release any additional pressure until float valve drops and then unlock lid. Ladle into bowls, garnish each bowl with a sprig of parsley, and serve warm.

Chive & Truffle Potato Mash

Servings: 4

Cooking Time: 35 Minutes

Ingredients:

- 1 lb potatoes, quartered
- ½ cup milk
- 2 tbsp truffle oil
- Salt and pepper to taste
- 2 tbsp chives, chopped

Directions:

1. Pour 1 cup of water into your Instant Pot and fit in a trivet. Place the potatoes on the trivet and seal the lid. Select Manual and cook for 15 minutes on High pressure.
2. Once over, allow a natural release for 10 minutes, then perform a quick pressure release, and unlock the lid. Remove potatoes to a bowl and mash them until smooth. Stir in milk and truffle oil; season with salt and pepper. Sprinkle with chives and serve.

Provençal Ratatouille

Servings: 4

Cooking Time: 20 Minutes

Ingredients:

- 2 tbsp olive oil
- 1 red onion, sliced
- 2 garlic cloves, minced
- 2 eggplants, sliced
- 3 zucchini, sliced
- ½ fennel bulb, sliced
- 2 red bell peppers, sliced
- 1 cup vegetable broth
- 14 oz canned tomatoes, diced
- ½ tbsp herbs de Provence

Directions:

1. Warm the olive oil in your Instant Pot on Sauté. Place the onion, garlic, eggplants, zucchini, fennel, and bell peppers and cook for 3-4 minutes. Stir in tomatoes, vegetable broth, and herbs de

Provence and seal the lid. Select Manual and cook for 5 minutes on High pressure. When done, perform a quick pressure release. Serve.

Modern Minestrone With Pancetta

Servings: 6

Cooking Time: 30 Minutes

Ingredients:

- 2 tbsp olive oil
- 2 oz pancetta, chopped
- 1 onion, diced
- 1 parsnip, chopped
- 2 carrots, cut into rounds
- 2 celery stalks
- 2 garlic cloves, minced
- 1 tbsp dried basil
- 1 tbsp dried thyme
- 1 tbsp dried oregano
- 6 cups vegetable broth
- 1 lb green beans, chopped
- 1 can diced tomatoes
- 1 can chickpeas
- 2 cups small shaped pasta
- Salt and pepper to taste
- ½ cup grated Parmesan

Directions:

1. Heat oil on Sauté. Add onion, carrots, garlic, pancetta, celery, and parsnip and cook for 5 minutes until they become soft. Stir in basil, oregano, beans, broth, tomatoes, pepper, salt, thyme, chickpeas, and pasta. Seal the lid and cook for 6 minutes on High Pressure. Release pressure naturally for 10 minutes. Carefully unlock the lid. Garnished with Parmesan cheese and serve.

One-pot Sausages With Peppers & Onions

Servings: 4

Cooking Time: 20 Minutes

Ingredients:

- 2 red bell peppers, cut into strips
- 4 pork sausages
- 1 sweet onion, sliced
- 1 tbsp olive oil
- ½ cup beef broth
- ¼ cup white wine
- 1 tsp garlic, minced
- Salt and pepper to taste

Directions:

1. On Sauté, add the sausages and brown them for a few minutes. Remove to a plate and discard the liquid. Press Cancel. Wipe clean the cooker and heat the oil on Sauté. Stir in onion and bell peppers. Stir-fry them for 5 minutes until soft. Add garlic and cook for a minute. Add the sausages and pour in broth and wine. Season with salt and pepper. Seal the lid and cook for 5 minutes on High pressure. Once done, do a quick pressure release. Serve.

Jalapeño-cheddar Hush Puppies

Servings:4

Cooking Time: 28 Minutes

Ingredients:

- 1 packet Martha White Hush Puppy Mix With Onion Flavor
- ¾ cup whole milk
- ¼ cup finely shredded Cheddar cheese
- 2 tablespoons grated yellow onion
- 1 large jalapeño, seeded and diced
- 1 cup water

Directions:

1. Grease a seven-hole silicone egg mold.
2. In a medium bowl, combine hush puppy mix and milk. Add cheese, onion, and jalapeño and stir to combine. Fill egg mold with half of batter. Cover egg mold with aluminum foil.
3. Add water to the Instant Pot and insert steam rack. Place filled egg mold on steam rack. Lock lid.
4. Press the Manual or Pressure Cook button and adjust time to 14 minutes. When timer beeps, quick-release pressure until float valve drops. Unlock lid.
5. Allow hush puppies to cool for 5 minutes, pop out of mold, and then transfer to a cooling rack. Repeat with remaining batter.
6. Serve warm.

Zucchini & Bacon Cheese Quiche

Servings: 4

Cooking Time: 40 Minutes

Ingredients:

- 4 slices cooked and crumbled bacon
- 1 zucchini, chopped
- 6 large eggs, beaten
- ½ cup milk
- Salt and pepper to taste
- 1 cup diced ham
- 1 cup Parmesan, shredded
- 2 spring onions, chopped

Directions:

1. Pour 1 cup of water into your Instant Pot and fit in a trivet. Mix eggs, milk, salt, and pepper in a bowl. Add in ham, bacon, zucchini, Parmesan cheese, and spring onions and stir. Cover with aluminum foil and place it on top of the trivet. Seal the lid, select Manual, and cook for 20 minutes on High pressure. When done, allow a natural release for 10 minutes and unlock the lid. Serve.

Corn Soup With Chicken & Egg

Servings: 2

Cooking Time: 25 Minutes

Ingredients:

- 1 tbsp cilantro, chopped
- 1 egg
- ½ lb chicken breasts
- 1 leek, chopped
- 1 tbsp sliced shallots
- ¼ tsp nutmeg
- 2 cups water
- ¼ cup corn kernels
- ¼ cup diced carrots
- Salt and pepper to taste

Directions:

1. Slice the chicken breasts into small cubes and place them in your Instant Pot. Add in corn kernels, water, shallots, salt, nutmeg, and black pepper. Seal the lid, select Pressure Cook, and cook for 15 minutes on High.
2. When done, allow a natural release and unlock the lid. Mix in carrots and leek and bring to a boil on Sauté. Beat the egg in a bowl. Once the Soup boil, pour in the beaten egg and toss until well combined and done. Divide between bowls, sprinkle with cilantro, and serve.

Broccoli Cheddar Soup

Servings:4

Cooking Time: 25 Minutes

Ingredients:

- 2 tablespoons butter
- 1 medium sweet onion, peeled and chopped
- 1 large carrot, peeled and chopped
- 2 cloves garlic, chopped
- 1 large bunch broccoli, coarsely chopped
- ½ cup chardonnay
- 3 cups chicken broth
- 1 teaspoon sea salt
- ½ teaspoon ground black pepper
- Pinch of ground nutmeg

- ½ cup whole milk
- 1 cup sharp Cheddar cheese

Directions:

1. Press the Sauté button on the Instant Pot and heat the butter. Add onion, carrot, and garlic. Sauté for 5 minutes until the onions are translucent. Add the broccoli. Continue to sauté for 3 minutes until broccoli starts to become tender. Add wine, broth, salt, pepper, and nutmeg. Press the Adjust button to change the temperature to Less and simmer for 5 minutes. Lock lid.
2. Press the Manual button and adjust time to 10 minutes. When timer beeps, quick-release pressure until float valve drops and then unlock lid.
3. Add milk and cheese. In the Instant Pot, purée the soup with an immersion blender, or use a stand blender and purée in batches.
4. Ladle into bowls and serve warm.

Turmeric Butternut Squash Soup

Servings: 4

Cooking Time: 40 Minutes

Ingredients:

- 1.5 lb butternut squash, peeled and chopped
- 1 onion, chopped
- 4 cups vegetable broth
- 1 tbsp ground turmeric
- ½ tbsp heavy cream
- Salt and pepper to taste
- 2 tbsp parsley, chopped
- 3 tbsp olive oil

Directions:

1. Heat oil on Sauté and stir-fry onion for 3 minutes. Add in butternut squash, turmeric, vegetable broth, salt, and pepper and stir well. Seal the lid. Press Soup/Broth and cook for 30 minutes on High. Do a quick release. With an immersion blender, blend until smooth. Stir in heavy cream and top with freshly chopped parsley. Serve warm.

Navy Bean & Zucchini Soup

Servings: 4

Cooking Time: 25 Minutes

Ingredients:

- 2 tbsp olive oil
- 1 onion, chopped
- 2 garlic cloves, minced
- 1 zucchini, chopped
- 1 carrot, chopped
- 1 celery stalk, chopped
- 1 cup canned navy beans
- 1 tsp fresh thyme
- 1 bay leaf
- 4 cups vegetable stock
- Salt and pepper to taste
- 2 tbsp parsley, chopped

Directions:

1. Warm the olive oil in your Instant Pot on Sauté. Add in onion and garlic and sweat for 4-5 minutes. Add in zucchini, carrot, and celery and cook for 5 more minutes.
2. Stir in beans, thyme, bay leaf, stock, salt, and pepper and seal the lid. Select Manual and cook for 8 minutes on High. When over, perform a quick pressure release. Discard bay leaf. Top with parsley and serve. Enjoy!

Minestrone With Fresh Herbs

Servings: 4

Cooking Time: 25 Minutes

Ingredients:

- 2 tbsp olive oil
- 1 large onion, diced
- 3 garlic cloves, minced
- 2 celery stalks, diced
- 1 carrot, diced
- 2 tsp basil, chopped
- 1 tsp oregano, chopped
- 1 tsp rosemary, chopped
- Salt and pepper to taste
- 14 oz can tomatoes, diced
- 5 curly kale, chopped
- ½ cup elbow macaroni
- 4 cups vegetable broth
- 14 oz can cannellini beans

Directions:

1. Warm the olive oil in your Instant Pot on Sauté. Add in onion, garlic, celery, and carrot and cook for 5 minutes until tender. Stir in basil, oregano, rosemary, tomatoes, elbow macaroni, cannellini beans, and vegetable broth.
2. Seal the lid, select Manual, and cook for 6 minutes on High. Once done, perform a quick pressure release. Unlock the lid. Stir in kale and press Sauté. Cook for 4-5 minutes until it's wilted. Taste and adjust the seasoning.

Spicy Cauliflower Cakes

Servings: 4

Cooking Time: 20 Minutes

Ingredients:

- 1 cauliflower head, chopped
- 1 cup panko breadcrumbs
- 1 cup Parmesan, shredded
- Salt and pepper to taste
- ½ tsp cayenne pepper
- 2 tbsp olive oil

Directions:

1. Pour 1 cup of water into your Instant Pot and fit in a steamer basket. Place in the cauliflower and seal the lid. Select Manual and cook for 3 minutes on High pressure.
2. Once ready, perform a quick pressure release and unlock the lid. Mash the cauliflower with a fork in a bowl. Add in breadcrumbs, Parmesan cheese, cayenne pepper, salt, and black pepper and mix to combine. Form the meat mixture into patties. Clean the pot and warm the olive oil on Sauté. Fry the cakes for 4-5 minutes, flipping once until golden brown. Serve warm.

Feta & Potato Salad

Servings: 4

Cooking Time: 25 Minutes + Chilling Time

Ingredients:

- 3 lb potatoes, chopped
- 1 cup mayonnaise
- ¼ cup mustard
- ¼ cup pickles
- 1 white onion, chopped
- 1 cup feta, crumbled

Directions:

1. Place the potatoes in your Instant Pot and cover them with water. Seal the lid and cook for 6 minutes on High Pressure. Once ready, do a natural release for 10 minutes. Drain the potatoes and allow to cool. Chop into small pieces. In a bowl, mix pickles, mayonnaise, potatoes, mustard, and onion. Top with feta cheese to serve.

Green Soup

Servings: 4

Cooking Time: 20 Minutes

Ingredients:

- 2 tbsp olive oil
- 1 onion, chopped
- 1 celery rib, chopped
- 10 oz broccoli florets
- 2 cups kale
- 4 cups chicken broth
- Salt and pepper to taste
- 2 tbsp peanut butter
- ¼ cup heavy cream

Directions:

1. Warm the olive oil in your Instant Pot on Sauté. Place the onion and cook for 3 minutes until translucent. Add in celery and broccoli and cook for another 2 minutes.
2. Pour in chicken broth and kale and seal the lid. Select Manual and cook for 5 minutes on High pressure. Once done, perform a quick pressure

release and unlock the lid. Let chill, then blend it. Stir in peanut butter and heavy cream and adjust the seasonings. Serve right away.

Chilled Pearl Couscous Salad

Servings:6

Cooking Time: 10 Minutes

Ingredients:

- 3 tablespoons olive oil, divided
- 1 cup pearl couscous
- 1 cup water
- 1 cup fresh orange juice
- 1 small cucumber, seeded and diced
- 1 small yellow bell pepper, seeded and diced
- 2 small Roma tomatoes, seeded and diced
- ¼ cup slivered almonds
- ¼ cup chopped fresh mint leaves
- 2 tablespoons lemon juice
- 1 teaspoon lemon zest
- ¼ cup feta cheese
- ¼ teaspoon fine sea salt
- 1 teaspoon smoked paprika
- 1 teaspoon garlic powder

Directions:

1. Press the Sauté button on the Instant Pot. Heat 1 tablespoon olive oil, add couscous, and stir-fry for 2–4 minutes until couscous is slightly browned. Add water and orange juice. Lock lid.
2. Press the Manual button and adjust time to 5 minutes. When the timer beeps, let pressure release naturally for 5 minutes. Quick-release any additional pressure until float valve drops and then unlock lid. Drain any liquid.
3. Combine remaining ingredients in a medium bowl. Set aside. Once couscous has cooled, toss it into bowl ingredients. Cover and refrigerate overnight until ready to serve chilled.

Four Cheeses Party Pizza

Servings: 4

Cooking Time: 25 Minutes

Ingredients:

- 1 pizza crust
- ½ cup tomato paste
- 1 tsp dried oregano
- 1 oz cheddar, grated
- 5-6 mozzarella slices
- ¼ cup grated gouda cheese
- ¼ cup grated Parmesan
- 2 tbsp olive oil

Directions:

1. Grease the bottom of a baking dish with 1 tbsp of olive oil. Line some parchment paper. Flour the working surface and roll out the pizza dough to the approximate size of your Instant Pot. Gently fit the dough in the previously prepared baking dish.
2. In a bowl, combine tomato paste with water and dried oregano. Spread the mixture over the dough and finish with cheeses. Add a trivet inside your the pot and Pour in 1 cup of water. Seal the lid, and cook for 15 minutes on High Pressure. Do a quick release. Remove the pizza from the pot using parchment paper. Cut and serve.

Spicy Tomato Soup With Rice

Servings: 4

Cooking Time: 55 Minutes

Ingredients:

- 1 cup tomato puree
- 1 onion, chopped
- 1 garlic clove, minced
- ¼ cup rice
- Salt and pepper to taste
- 2 tbsp olive oil
- 4 cups vegetable broth
- ¼ tsp cayenne pepper
- 1 tsp basil, chopped

Directions:

1. Heat oil on Sauté and cook garlic and onion 3 minutes until soft. Add in tomato puree, rice, vegetable broth, and cayenne pepper. Season with salt and black pepper. Seal the lid and cook on Soup/Broth for 30 minutes on High Pressure. Release the pressure naturally for about 10 minutes. Serve in bowls sprinkled with basil.

Broccoli & Mushroom Egg Cups

Servings: 6

Cooking Time: 15 Minutes

Ingredients:

- 1 tsp dried oregano
- 10 eggs
- 1 cup Pecorino cheese, grated
- 1 cup heavy cream
- 4 oz broccoli florets
- 1 onion, chopped
- 1 cup sliced mushrooms
- 1 tbsp chopped parsley
- Salt and pepper to taste

Directions:

1. Pour 1 cup of water into your Instant Pot and fit in a trivet. In a bowl, whisk the eggs and heavy cream. Mix in Pecorino cheese, broccoli, onion, oregano, mushrooms, parsley, salt, and black pepper. Divide the egg mixture between small jars and seal the lids. Place them on the trivet and seal the lid. Select Manual and cook for 5 minutes on High pressure. When done, perform a quick pressure release and unlock the lid. Remove the jars carefully and serve.

Italian-style Mustard Greens

Servings: 6

Cooking Time: 10 Minutes

Ingredients:

- 2 pounds mustard greens, chopped (spines removed)
- 1 small sweet onion, peeled and diced
- 1 cup chicken broth
- ¼ cup red wine vinegar
- ⅛ teaspoon red pepper flakes
- 2 teaspoons Italian seasoning
- 1 slice bacon
- ½ teaspoon salt
- ¼ teaspoon ground black pepper

Directions:

1. Place all ingredients in the Instant Pot. Lock lid.
2. Press the Manual or Pressure Cook button and adjust time to 10 minutes. When timer beeps, let pressure release naturally until float valve drops. Unlock lid. Discard bacon.
3. Using a slotted spoon, transfer mustard greens to a serving dish. Serve warm.

Wild Mushroom Soup

Servings: 4

Cooking Time: 25 Minutes

Ingredients:

- 3 tablespoons unsalted butter
- 1 small sweet onion, peeled and diced
- 2 cups sliced mushrooms (shiitake, cremini, portobello, etc.)
- 4 cups chicken broth
- 1 tablespoon Italian seasoning
- 1 teaspoon salt
- ½ teaspoon ground black pepper
- 1 cup heavy cream
- 2 teaspoons cooking sherry

Directions:

1. Press the Sauté button on the Instant Pot. Add butter and heat until melted, then add onion. Sauté 3–5 minutes until onions are translucent.
2. Add mushrooms, broth, Italian seasoning, salt, and pepper. Press the Cancel button. Lock lid.
3. Press the Soup button and adjust time to 20 minutes. When timer beeps, let pressure release naturally for 10 minutes. Quick-release any additional pressure until float valve drops. Unlock lid.
4. Add cream and sherry. Use an immersion blender directly in pot to blend soup until desired consistency is reached, either chunky or smooth.
5. Ladle soup into bowls. Serve warm.

Cauliflower Cheese Soup

Servings: 4

Cooking Time: 30 Minutes

Ingredients:

- 2 tbsp butter
- 1 onion, diced
- 2 garlic cloves, minced
- 2 russet potatoes, chopped
- 5 oz cauliflower florets
- 4 cups vegetable broth
- 1 cup heavy cream
- 1 tsp mustard powder
- 1 cup cheddar, shredded
- 1 green onion, chopped
- Salt and pepper to taste

Directions:

1. Melt the butter in your Instant Pot on Sauté. Add in onion and garlic and cook for 2-3 minutes until lightly golden. Add in potato, cauliflower, mustard powder, vegetable broth, and give it a good stir.
2. Seal the lid, select Manual, and cook for 8 minutes on High. Once over, allow a natural release for 10 minutes and unlock the lid. Stir in heavy cream and half of the cheddar cheese and whizz until smooth, using a stick blender. Adjust the seasoning. Scatter the remaining cheddar on top and sprinkle with green onion to serve.

Coconut & Cauliflower Curry

Servings: 4

Cooking Time: 25 Minutes

Ingredients:

- 2 tbsp butter
- 1 onion, chopped
- 3 cups chicken broth
- 1 cup coconut milk
- 2 tbsp red curry paste
- ½ tsp cardamom
- ½ tsp cumin
- 1 head cauliflower, chopped
- 1 tbsp cilantro, chopped

Directions:

1. Melt the butter in your Instant Pot on Sauté. Place the onion and cook for 4-5 minutes. Add in chicken broth, cauliflower, coconut milk, curry paste, cardamon, and cumin and seal the lid. Select Manual and cook for 10 minutes on High pressure. When ready, perform a quick pressure release and unlock the lid. Blend the soup using an immersion blender. Serve topped cilantro.

Crushed Potatoes With Aioli

Servings: 4

Cooking Time: 25 Minutes

Ingredients:

- 1 lb Russet potatoes, pierced
- Salt and pepper to taste
- 2 tbsp olive oil
- 4 tbsp mayonnaise
- 1 tsp garlic paste
- 1 tbsp lemon juice

Directions:

1. Mix the olive oil, salt, and pepper in a bowl. Add in the potatoes and toss to coat. Pour 1 cup of water into your Instant Pot and fit in a trivet. Place the potatoes on the trivet and seal the lid. Select Manual and cook for 12 minutes on High. Once ready, perform a quick release.

2. In a small bowl, combine the mayonnaise, garlic paste, and lemon juice and whisk well. Peel and crush the potatoes and transfer to a serving bowl. Serve with aioli.

Asparagus & Tomato Tart

Servings: 4

Cooking Time: 40 Minutes

Ingredients:

- 10 eggs
- ½ cup milk
- Salt and pepper to taste
- 1 lb chopped asparagus
- 1 cup tomatoes, chopped
- 4 green onions, chopped
- 3 tomato slices
- ¼ cup Parmesan, shredded

Directions:

1. Crack the eggs in a bowl and beat them with milk, salt, and pepper. In a separated bowl, mix asparagus, chopped tomatoes, and green onions and transfer to a baking dish. Pour the egg mixture over and toss to combine. Top with tomato slices and Parmesan cheese. Pour 1 cup of water into your Instant Pot and fit in a trivet.

2. Place the dish on top of the trivet and seal the lid. Select Manual and cook for 20 minutes on High pressure. Once ready, allow a natural release for 10 minutes, then perform a quick pressure release, and unlock the lid. Serve warm.

Beans, Rice, & Grains

Beans, Rice, & Grains

Kale & Parmesan Pearl Barley

Servings: 2

Cooking Time: 30 Minutes

Ingredients:

- 1 tbsp butter
- 1 small onion, diced
- 1 cup pearl barley
- 2 garlic cloves, smashed
- 2 cups vegetable broth
- ½ cup grated Parmesan
- 1 cup kale, chopped
- ½ lemon, juiced

Directions:

1. Warm butter on Sauté. Add in onion and cook for 3 minutes until soft. Stir in garlic and barley and continue cooking for 1 to 2 minutes. Mix in broth and season. Seal the lid and cook for 9 minutes on High Pressure. Release pressure naturally for 10 minutes. Add in Parmesan cheese and kale and stir until the cheese is fully melted. Drizzle with lemon juice and serve.

Pomegranate Rice With Vegetables

Servings: 4

Cooking Time: 15 Minutes

Ingredients:

- ¼ cup pomegranate seeds
- 2 tbsp olive oil
- 1 onion, finely chopped
- 2 cloves garlic, minced
- 1 cup basmati rice
- 1 cup sweet corn, frozen
- 1 cup garden peas, frozen
- ¼ tsp salt
- 1 tsp turmeric powder

- 1 ¼ cups vegetable stock

Directions:

1. Warm oil your Instant Pot on Sauté and add onion and garlic; cook for 3 minutes until fragrant. Stir in rice, corn, peas, salt, turmeric, and stock. Seal the lid, select Manual, and cook for 4 minutes on High pressure. When ready, perform a quick pressure release and unlock the lid. With a fork, fluff the rice. Top with pomegranate and serve.

Basic Risotto

Servings: 4

Cooking Time: 19 Minutes

Ingredients:

- 4 tablespoons unsalted butter
- 1 small yellow onion, peeled and finely diced
- 2 cloves garlic, peeled and minced
- 1 ½ cups Arborio rice
- 4 cups chicken broth, divided
- 3 tablespoons grated Parmesan cheese
- ½ teaspoon salt
- ¼ teaspoon ground black pepper

Directions:

1. Press the Sauté button on the Instant Pot. Add butter and heat until melted. Add onion and stir-fry 3–5 minutes until onions are translucent. Add garlic and rice and cook an additional 1 minute.
2. Add 1 cup broth and stir 2–3 minutes until it is absorbed by rice.
3. Add remaining 3 cups broth, cheese, salt, and pepper. Press the Cancel button. Lock lid.
4. Press the Manual or Pressure Cook button and adjust time to 10 minutes. When timer beeps, let pressure release naturally for 10 minutes. Quick-release any additional pressure until float valve drops. Unlock lid.
5. Ladle risotto into bowls. Serve warm.

Barley & Smoked Salmon Salad

Servings: 4

Cooking Time: 30 Minutes

Ingredients:

- 4 smoked salmon fillets, flaked
- 1 cup pearl barley
- Salt and pepper to taste
- 1 cup arugula
- 1 green apple, chopped

Directions:

1. Place the barley, 2 cups of water, salt, and pepper in your Instant Pot. Seal the lid, select Manual, and cook for 20 minutes on High pressure.
2. Once ready, perform a quick pressure release and unlock the lid. Remove barley to a serving bowl. Mix in apple and salmon. Top with arugula.

Hazelnut Brown Rice Pilaf

Servings: 4

Cooking Time: 45 Minutes

Ingredients:

- ¼ cup hazelnuts, toasted and chopped
- 2 tbsp olive oil
- 1 cup brown rice
- 2 cups vegetable broth
- Salt and pepper to taste

Directions:

1. Place the rice, vegetable broth, olive oil, pepper, and salt in your Instant Pot and stir. Seal the lid, select Manual, and cook for 25 minutes on High. Once ready, allow a natural release for 10 minutes and unlock the lid. Using a fork, fluff the rice. Top with hazelnuts and serve.

Easy Brown Rice With Sunflower Seeds

Servings: 6

Cooking Time: 30 Minutes

Ingredients:

- 1 tbsp toasted sunflower seeds
- 1 ½ cups brown rice
- 3 cups chicken broth
- 2 tsp lemon juice
- 2 tsp olive oil
- Salt and pepper to taste

Directions:

1. Add broth and brown rice. Season with salt and black pepper. Seal the lid, press Manual, and cook on High for 15 minutes. Release the pressure quickly. Do not open the lid for 5 minutes. Use a fork to fluff rice. Add lemon juice, sunflower seeds, and a drizzle of olive oil and serve.

Spinach & Anchovy Fusilli

Servings: 4

Cooking Time: 15 Minutes

Ingredients:

- 1 lb fusilli pasta
- 4 cups spinach, chopped
- 4 anchovy fillets, chopped
- ½ cup Parmesan, shredded
- 2 tbsp butter
- ½ tsp grated nutmeg
- 3 tbsp pine nuts, toasted
- Salt and pepper to taste

Directions:

1. Place fusilli pasta and 4 cups of salted water in your Instant Pot and seal the lid. Select Manual and cook for 4 minutes on High. When done, perform a quick pressure release and unlock the lid. Drain the pasta, reserving 1 cup of the liquid and set aside. Melt butter on Sauté
2. Add in spinach. Stir for 2 minutes and pour in the pasta liquid. Return the pasta, stir in anchovies, nutmeg, and pine nuts. Adjust the taste. Top with Parmesan and serve.

Chorizo & Lentil Stew

Servings: 4

Cooking Time: 60 Minutes

Ingredients:

- 1 cups lentils
- 4 oz chorizo, chopped
- 1 onion, diced
- 2 garlic cloves, minced
- 2 cups tomato sauce
- 2 cups vegetable broth
- ½ cup mustard
- ½ cup cider vinegar
- 3 tbsp Worcestershire sauce
- 2 tbsp maple syrup
- 2 tbsp liquid smoke
- 1 tbsp lime juice
- 2 cups brown sugar
- Salt and pepper to taste
- 1 tsp chili powder
- 1 tsp paprika
- ¼ tsp cayenne pepper

Directions:

1. Set to Sauté the Instant Pot. Add in chorizo and cook for 3 minutes as you stir until crisp. Add garlic and onion and cook for 2 minutes. Mix in tomato sauce, cider vinegar, liquid smoke, Worcestershire sauce, lime juice, mustard, and maple syrup and cook for 2 minutes.
2. Stir in broth and scrape the bottom to do away with any browned bits of food. Add pepper, chili, sugar, paprika, salt, and cayenne into the sauce as you stir to mix.
3. Stir in lentils to coat. Seal the lid and cook on High Pressure for 30 minutes. Release pressure naturally for 10 minutes and unlock the lid. Serve warm.

Black Beans With Jalapeño Salsa

Servings: 4

Cooking Time: 50 Minutes

Ingredients:

- 2 tbsp olive oil
- 1 cup black beans, soaked
- 3 cups veggie broth
- 1 onion, quartered
- 1 tsp cumin
- Salt and pepper to taste
- ½ cup Jalapeno-cilantro salsa

Directions:

1. Warm the olive oil in your Instant Pot. Place in onion and cook for 3 minutes. Stir in black beans, veggie broth, cumin, salt, and pepper. Seal the lid, select Manual, and cook for 25 minutes on High pressure. When ready, allow a natural release for 10 minutes and unlock the lid. Drizzle with Jalapeño-Cilantro Salsa and serve.

Chicken & Broccoli Fettuccine Alfredo

Servings: 2

Cooking Time: 15 Minutes

Ingredients:

- 1 cup cooked chicken breasts, chopped
- 1 cup broccoli florets
- 8 oz fettuccine, halved
- 1 tsp chicken seasoning
- 1 jar Alfredo sauce
- Salt and pepper to taste
- 1 tbsp parsley, chopped
- 1 tbsp Parmesan, grated

Directions:

1. Add 2 cups of water, fettuccine, and chicken seasoning to your Instant Pot. Place a steamer basket on top and add in the broccoli. Seal the lid, select Manual, and cook for 3 minutes on High. Once over, perform a quick pressure release. Drain the pasta and set aside. In a bowl, place Alfredo sauce, broccoli, parsley, and cooked chicken. Add in the pasta and mix to combine. Season with salt and pepper. Serve topped with Parmesan cheese.

Green Goddess Mac 'n' Cheese

Servings: 4

Cooking Time: 20 Minutes

Ingredients:

- 2 cups kale, chopped
- 2 tbsp cilantro, chopped
- 16 oz elbow macaroni
- 3 tbsp unsalted butter
- 4 cups chicken broth
- 3 cups mozzarella, grated
- ½ cup Parmesan, shredded
- ½ cup sour cream

Directions:

1. Mix the macaroni, butter, and chicken broth in your Instant Pot and seal the lid. Select Manual and cook for 4 minutes on High. When ready, perform a quick pressure release and unlock the lid. Stir in Parmesan and mozzarella cheeses, sour cream, kale, and cilantro. Put the lid and let sit for 5 minutes until the kale wilts. Serve.

Creamy Polenta

Servings: 6

Cooking Time: 15 Minutes

Ingredients:

- 3 cups water
- 1 cup whole milk
- 1 cup coarse ground yellow polenta
- 1 teaspoon salt
- ¼ teaspoon ground black pepper
- 2 tablespoons unsalted butter
- ¼ cup grated Parmesan cheese

Directions:

1. Add water, milk, polenta, salt, and pepper to the Instant Pot and stir. Lock lid.
2. Press the Manual or Pressure Cook button and adjust time to 10 minutes. When timer beeps, quick-release pressure until float valve drops. Unlock lid.
3. Whisk butter and cheese into polenta in pot up to

5 minutes until it thickens.

4. Transfer polenta to a serving dish. Serve warm.

Millet Tabouleh

Servings: 4

Cooking Time: 10 Minutes

Ingredients:

- 1½ cups chopped fresh parsley
- ¼ cup chopped fresh mint leaves
- 1 cup peeled and diced red onion
- ¼ cup small-diced zucchini
- ½ cup peeled, seeded, and small-diced cucumber
- 4 small Roma tomatoes, seeded and diced
- ¼ cup plus 2 teaspoons olive oil, divided
- ¼ cup lemon juice
- 1 teaspoon lemon zest
- 1½ teaspoons sea salt, divided
- ¼ teaspoon ground black pepper
- 1 cup millet
- 2 cups vegetable broth

Directions:

1. In a medium bowl, combine parsley, mint, onion, zucchini, cucumber, tomatoes, ¼ cup olive oil, lemon juice, lemon zest, 1 teaspoon salt, and pepper. Cover and refrigerate for 30 minutes up to overnight.
2. Drizzle 2 teaspoons olive oil in Instant Pot. Add millet to Instant Pot in an even layer. Add broth and remaining ½ teaspoon salt. Lock lid.
3. Press the Rice button. When the timer beeps, let pressure release naturally for 5 minutes. Quick-release any additional pressure until float valve drops and then unlock lid.
4. Transfer millet to a serving bowl and set aside to cool. When cooled, add to refrigerated mixture and stir. Serve.

Couscous With Lamb & Vegetables

Servings: 4

Cooking Time: 40 Minutes

Ingredients:

- 2 tbsp olive oil
- 1 large onion, chopped
- 2 garlic cloves, minced
- 1 lb lamb stew meat, cubed
- 3 cups vegetable stock
- 1 carrot, grated
- 1 red bell pepper, chopped
- 1 cup Israeli couscous
- ½ tsp cumin
- Salt and pepper to taste
- 2 tbsp cilantro, chopped
- 4 lemon wedges

Directions:

1. Heat olive oil on Sauté and cook onion, garlic, and lamb for 6-7 minutes. Stir in carrot, bell pepper, and cumin and sauté for another 3 minutes. Pour in vegetable stock and adjust the seasoning with salt and pepper. Close and secure the lid. Select Manual and cook for 10 minutes on High. Once cooking is complete, use a natural release.
2. Add the couscous and select Sauté on Low. Cover with the lid and simmer for 8-10 minutes until the couscous is tender. Select Cancel and let it sit for 2-3 minutes. Fluff and top with cilantro. Serve with lemon wedges.

Rice & Red Bean Pot

Servings: 4

Cooking Time: 55 Minutes

Ingredients:

- 1 cup red beans, soaked
- 2 tbsp vegetable oil
- ½ cup rice
- ½ tbsp cayenne pepper
- 1 ½ cups vegetable broth
- 1 onion, diced
- 1 garlic clove, minced
- 1 red bell pepper, diced
- 1 stalk celery, diced
- Salt and pepper to taste

Directions:

1. Place beans in your Instant Pot with enough water to cover them by a couple of fingers. Seal the lid and cook for 25 minutes on High Pressure. Release the pressure quickly. Drain the beans and set aside.
2. Rinse and pat dry the inner pot. Add in oil and press Sauté. Add in onion and garlic and sauté for 3 minutes until soft. Add celery and bell pepper and cook for 2 minutes.
3. Add in the rice, reserved beans, vegetable broth. Stir in pepper, cayenne pepper, and salt. Seal the lid and cook for 15 minutes on High Pressure. Release the pressure quickly. Carefully unlock the lid. Serve warm.

Creamy Fettuccine With Ground Beef

Servings: 6

Cooking Time: 20 Minutes

Ingredients:

- 10 oz ground beef
- 1 lb fettuccine pasta
- 1 cup cheddar, shredded
- 1 cup fresh spinach, torn
- 1 medium onion, chopped
- 2 cups tomatoes, diced
- 1 tbsp butter
- Salt and pepper to taste

Directions:

1. Melt butter on Sauté. Stir-fry the beef and onion for 5 minutes. Add the pasta. Pour water enough to cover and season with salt and pepper. Cook on High Pressure for 5 minutes. Do a quick release. Press Sauté and stir in the tomatoes and spinach. Cook for 5 minutes. Top with shredded cheddar and serve.

Spinach, Garlic & Mushroom Pilaf

Servings: 6

Cooking Time: 45 Minutes

Ingredients:

- 2 cups button mushrooms, sliced
- 1 tbsp olive oil
- 2 cloves garlic, minced
- 1 onion, chopped
- 1 cup spinach, chopped
- 4 cups vegetable stock
- 2 cups white rice
- 1 tsp salt
- 2 sprigs parsley, chopped

Directions:

1. Select Sauté and heat oil. Add mushrooms, onion, and garlic, and stir-fry for 5 minutes until tender. Mix in rice, stock, spinach, and salt. Seal the lid and cook on High Pressure for 20 minutes. Release pressure naturally for 10 minutes. Fluff the rice and top with parsley. Serve.

Risotto With Broccoli & Grana Padano

Servings: 6

Cooking Time: 35 Minutes

Ingredients:

- 2 tbsp Grana Padano cheese flakes
- 10 oz broccoli florets
- 1 onion, chopped
- 3 tbsp butter
- 2 cups carnaroli rice, rinsed
- ¼ cup dry white wine
- 4 cups chicken stock
- Salt and pepper to taste
- 2 tbsp Grana Padano, grated

Directions:

1. Warm butter on Sauté. Stir-fry onion for 3 minutes until translucent. Add in broccoli and rice and cook for 5 minutes, stirring occasionally. Pour wine into the pot and scrape away any browned bits of food from the pan.
2. Stir in stock, pepper, and salt. Seal the lid, press Manual and cook on High for 15 minutes. Release the pressure quickly. Sprinkle with grated Grana Padano cheese and stir well. Top with flaked Grana Padano cheese to serve.

Tomato & Mushroom Rotini

Servings: 4

Cooking Time: 35 Minutes

Ingredients:

- 1 lb rotini pasta
- 2 tbsp olive oil
- ½ yellow onion, diced
- 2 garlic cloves, minced
- 16 oz crushed tomatoes
- 1 cup Mushrooms, sliced
- ½ tbsp grated nutmeg
- ¼ cup basil, chopped
- Salt and pepper to taste

Directions:

1. Cover rotini pasta with salted water in your Instant Pot and seal the lid. Select Manual and cook for 4 minutes on High. When done, allow a natural release for 10 minutes, then perform a quick pressure release, and unlock the lid. Drain the pasta and transfer to a bowl.
2. Heat the olive oil on Sauté and cook the onion, mushrooms, and garlic for 3-4 minutes. Stir in tomatoes and nutmeg and simmer for 5-6 minutes. Stir in basil and cooked pasta; adjust the seasoning. Serve.

South American Pot

Servings: 4

Cooking Time: 30 Minutes

Ingredients:

- 1 cups brown rice
- ½ cup soaked black beans
- 1 tbsp tomato paste
- 1 garlic clove, minced
- 2 tsp onion powder
- 2 tsp chili powder
- Salt to taste
- ¼ tsp cumin
- 1 tsp hot paprika
- 3 cups corn kernels

Directions:

1. Place rice, beans, 4 cups water, tomato paste, garlic, onion powder, chili powder, salt, cumin, paprika, and corn in your Instant Pot and stir. Seal the lid, select Manual, and cook for 20 minutes on High pressure. Once ready, perform a quick pressure release and unlock the lid. Adjust the seasoning. Serve immediately.

Red Pepper & Chicken Fusilli

Servings: 2

Cooking Time: 15 Minutes

Ingredients:

- 8 oz fusilli pasta
- 1 cup tomato pasta sauce
- 1 tbsp paprika
- 1 red bell pepper, sliced
- 2 chicken breasts, sliced
- 2 garlic cloves, chopped
- ½ tsp Italian seasoning
- Salt and red pepper to taste
- 1 tbsp butter
- 1 cup Parmesan, grated

Directions:

1. Stir 1 cup of water, fusilli, and pasta sauce in your Instant Pot. Add in chicken breasts, garlic, red

pepper, Italian seasoning, paprika, salt, and pepper and seal the lid. Select Manual and cook for 5 minutes on High. Once over, perform a quick pressure release and unlock the lid. Stir in butter and top with Parmesan cheese to serve.

Fusilli With Chicken Bolognese Sauce

Servings: 4

Cooking Time: 50 Minutes

Ingredients:

- 2 tbsp olive oil
- 6 oz bacon, cubed
- 1 onion, minced
- 1 carrot, minced
- 1 celery stalk, minced
- 2 garlic cloves, crushed
- ¼ cup tomato paste
- ¼ tbsp red pepper flakes
- 1 ½ lb ground chicken
- ½ cup white wine
- 1 cup milk
- 1 cup chicken broth
- Salt to taste
- 1 lb fusilli pasta

Directions:

1. Warm olive oil on Sauté. Add in bacon and fry for 5 minutes. Add celery, carrot, garlic, and onion and cook for 5 minutes. Mix in red pepper flakes and tomato paste, and cook for 2 minutes. Break chicken into small pieces and place them in the pot. Cook for 10 minutes as you stir until browned. Pour in the wine and simmer for 2 minutes. Add in chicken broth, salt, and milk.

2. Seal the lid and cook for 15 minutes on High Pressure. Release the pressure quickly. Add in the fusilli and stir. Seal the lid, and cook on High Pressure for another 5 minutes. Release the pressure quickly. Serve.

Chili Mac & Cheese

Servings: 6

Cooking Time: 15 Minutes

Ingredients:

- 2 cups Pecorino Romano cheese, grated
- 12 oz macaroni
- 4 cups cold water
- Salt and pepper to taste
- 2 eggs
- 1 tbsp chili powder
- 4 tbsp butter
- 1 ½ cups milk
- 4 cups cheddar, grated

Directions:

1. Add salt, water, and macaroni. Seal the lid and cook for 4 minutes on High Pressure. Take a bowl and beat eggs, chili powder, and black pepper to mix well. Release the pressure quickly. Add butter to the pasta and stir until it melts. Stir in milk and egg mixture. Pour in Pecorino Romano and cheddar cheeses until melted. Cook in batches, if needed. Season to taste. Serve warm.

Black Bean Sliders

Servings:8

Cooking Time: 50 Minutes

Ingredients:

- 1 cup dried black beans
- 1 tablespoon olive oil
- 1 slice bacon
- 1 small red bell pepper, seeded and diced small
- 2 cups vegetable broth
- ½ teaspoon garlic powder
- ¼ teaspoon coriander
- ½ teaspoon chili powder
- ½ teaspoon ground cumin
- ½ teaspoon sea salt
- ¼ cup chopped fresh cilantro
- 1 large egg
- 1 cup panko bread crumbs
- 16 slider buns

Directions:

1. Rinse and drain beans.
2. Press the Sauté button on Instant Pot and heat olive oil. Add bacon and bell pepper. Stir-fry 3–5 minutes until bacon is cooked. Add broth and deglaze the Instant Pot by scraping the sides and bottom of the Instant Pot.
3. Add beans, garlic powder, coriander, chili powder, cumin, salt, and cilantro. Lock lid.
4. Press the Bean button and cook for the default time of 30 minutes. When timer beeps, let pressure release naturally for 10 minutes. Quick-release any additional pressure until float valve drops and then unlock lid.
5. Discard bacon. Press the Sauté button on the Instant Pot, press the Adjust button to change the heat to Less, and simmer bean mixture unlidded for 10 minutes to thicken. Remove mixture to a large bowl. Once cool enough to handle, quickly mix in egg and bread crumbs.
6. Form into 16 equal-sized small patties. Cook on stovetop in a skillet for approximately 2–3 minutes per side until browned.
7. Remove from heat and add each patty to a bun. Serve warm.

Lentil & Chorizo Chili

Servings: 4

Cooking Time: 40 Minutes

Ingredients:

- ½ lb chorizo sausage, sliced
- 2 tbsp olive oil
- 1 onion, diced
- 1 cup canned diced tomatoes
- 1 cup lentils
- 3 cups vegetable broth

Directions:

1. Warm the olive oil in your Instant Pot on Sauté. Place in onion and chorizo and sauté for 5 minutes. Add in tomatoes and cook for 1 more minute. Stir in lentils and vegetable broth. Seal the lid, select Manual, and cook for 15 minutes on High pressure. When ready, allow a natural release for 10 minutes and unlock the lid. Serve.

Arugula & Wild Mushroom Risotto

Servings: 4

Cooking Time: 30 Minutes

Ingredients:

- ½ cup wild mushrooms, chopped
- 4 tbsp pumpkin seeds, toasted
- 1/3 cup grated Pecorino Romano cheese
- 2 tbsp olive oil
- 1 onion, chopped
- 2 cups arugula, chopped
- 1 cup arborio rice
- 1/3 cup white wine
- 3 cups vegetable stock

Directions:

1. Heat oil on Sauté and cook onion and mushrooms for 5 minutes until tender. Add the rice and cook for a minute. Stir in white wine and cook for 2-3 minutes until almost evaporated. Pour in the stock. Seal the lid and cook on High Pressure for 10 minutes. Do a quick release. Stir in arugula and Pecorino Romano cheese to melt and serve scattered with pumpkin seeds.

Primavera Egg Noodles

Servings: 4

Cooking Time: 20 Minutes

Ingredients:

- 1 lb asparagus, trimmed
- 2 cups broccoli florets
- 3 tbsp olive oil
- Salt to taste
- 10 oz egg noodles
- 2 garlic cloves, minced
- 2 ½ cups vegetable stock
- ½ cup heavy cream
- 1 cup small tomatoes, halved
- ¼ cup chopped basil
- ½ cup grated Parmesan

Directions:

1. Pour the noodles, vegetable stock, and 2 tbsp olive oil, garlic, and salt in your Instant Pot. Place a trivet over. Combine asparagus, broccoli, remaining olive oil, stock, and salt in a bowl. Place the vegetables on the trivet. Seal the lid. Cook on Manual for 12 minutes.
2. Do a quick release. Remove the vegetables. Stir the heavy cream and tomatoes in the pasta. Press Sauté and simmer the cream for 2 minutes. Mix in asparagus and broccoli. Garnish with basil and Parmesan and serve.

Bell Pepper & Pinto Bean Stew

Servings: 6

Cooking Time: 55 Minutes

Ingredients:

- 2 tbsp olive oil
- 1 onion, chopped
- 1 red bell pepper, chopped
- 1 tbsp dried oregano
- 1 tbsp ground cumin
- 1 tsp red pepper flakes
- 3 cups vegetable stock
- 2 cups pinto beans, soaked
- 14 oz can tomatoes, diced
- 1 tbsp white wine vinegar
- ½ cup chives, chopped
- ¼ cup fresh corn kernels

Directions:

1. Set to Sauté your Instant Pot and heat oil. Stir in bell pepper, pepper flakes, oregano, onion, and cumin. Cook for 3 minutes. Mix in pinto beans, stock, and tomatoes. Seal the lid, select Manual, and cook for 30 minutes on High Pressure. Release the pressure naturally for 10 minutes. Add in vinegar. Divide among serving plates and top with corn and fresh chives to serve.

Four-cheese Traditional Italian Pasta

Servings: 6

Cooking Time: 20 Minutes

Ingredients:

- ¼ cup goat cheese, chopped
- ¼ cup grated Pecorino
- ½ cup grated Parmesan
- 1 cup heavy cream
- ½ cup grated gouda cheese
- ¼ cup butter, softened
- 1 tbsp Italian seasoning mix
- 1 cup vegetable broth
- 1 lb tagliatelle pasta

Directions:

1. Place the tagliatelle in your Instant Pot and cover with water. Seal the lid and cook on Manual for 4 minutes. Drain and set aside. In the pot, mix goat cheese, heavy cream, gouda cheese, broth, butter, and Italian seasoning. Press Sauté and cook for 4 minutes. Stir in the tagliatelle and Pecorino cheese and let simmer for 2 minutes. Top with Parmesan cheese and serve.

Pasta Caprese With Ricotta & Basil

Servings: 4

Cooking Time: 15 Minutes

Ingredients:

- 1 tbsp olive oil
- 1 onion, chopped
- 2 garlic cloves, minced
- 1 tbsp red pepper flakes
- 2 ½ cups fusilli pasta
- 1 can tomato sauce
- 1 cup cherry tomatoes, halved
- 1 cup water
- ¼ cup basil leaves
- 1 tbsp salt
- 1 cup ricotta, crumbled
- 2 tbsp chopped fresh basil

Directions:

1. Warm olive oil on Sauté. Add in red pepper flakes, garlic, and onion and cook for 3 minutes until soft. Mix in fusilli, tomatoes, basil, water, tomato sauce, and salt. Seal the lid, and cook on High Pressure for 4 minutes. Release the pressure quickly. Transfer the pasta to a serving platter and top with the crumbled cheese and remaining chopped basil.

Provençal Rice

Servings: 6

Cooking Time: 45 Minutes

Ingredients:

- 2 tbsp butter
- 1 onion, diced
- 2 garlic cloves, minced
- 2 cups brown rice
- 3 cups vegetable stock
- 1 tsp herbs de Provence
- 3 anchovy fillets, finely chopped
- 6 pitted Kalamata olives

Directions:

1. Melt butter in your Instant Pot on Sauté and add in onion and garlic; cook for 3 minutes. Stir in rice and herbs for 1 minute and pour in the stock. Seal the lid, select Manual, and cook for 22 minutes on High. When ready, allow a natural release for 10 minutes and unlock the lid. Stir in anchovy fillets. Serve topped with Kalamata olives.

Vegan & Vegetarian

Vegan & Vegetarian

Spinach Tagliatelle With Mushrooms

Servings: 4

Cooking Time: 25 Minutes

Ingredients:

- 8 oz spinach tagliatelle
- 6 oz mixed mushrooms
- 3 tbsp butter
- ¼ cup feta cheese
- ¼ cup grated Parmesan
- 2 garlic cloves, crushed
- ¼ cup heavy cream
- 1 tbsp Italian seasoning

Directions:

1. Melt butter on Sauté and stir-fry the garlic for a minute. Stir in feta, Italian seasoning, and mushrooms. Add the tagliatelle, 2 cups water, and heavy cream. Cook on High Pressure for 4 minutes. Quick-release the pressure. Top with Parmesan cheese. Serve and enjoy!

Quinoa With Brussels Sprouts & Broccoli

Servings: 2

Cooking Time: 25 Minutes

Ingredients:

- 1 cup quinoa, rinsed
- Salt and pepper to taste
- 1 beet, peeled, cubed
- 1 cup broccoli florets
- 1 carrot, chopped
- ½ lb Brussels sprouts
- 2 eggs
- 1 avocado, chopped
- ¼ cup pesto sauce
- Lemon wedges, for serving

Directions:

1. In the pot, mix 2 cups of water, salt, quinoa and pepper. Set trivet over quinoa and set steamer basket on top. To the steamer basket, add eggs, Brussels sprouts, broccoli, beet cubes, carrots, pepper, and salt. Seal the lid and cook for 1 minute on High Pressure. Release pressure naturally for 10 minutes. Remove the steamer basket and trivet from the pot and set the eggs in a bowl of ice water. Peel and halve the eggs. Use a fork to fluff the quinoa. Divide quinoa, broccoli, avocado, carrots, beet, Brussels sprouts, eggs between two bowls, and top with a pesto dollop. Serve with lemon wedges.

Butter Parmesan Zoodles

Servings:2

Cooking Time: 4 Minutes

Ingredients:

- 3 tablespoons unsalted butter, divided
- 4 medium zucchini, spiraled into "zoodles"
- ¼ cup grated vegetarian Parmesan cheese
- ¼ teaspoon salt
- ¼ teaspoon ground black pepper
- ¼ cup chopped fresh parsley

Directions:

1. Press the Sauté button on the Instant Pot. Add 2 tablespoons butter and heat until melted. Add "zoodles" and toss 3–4 minutes until softened.
2. Add remaining butter, cheese, salt, and pepper and toss in pot until butter is melted.
3. Transfer to bowls and garnish with parsley. Serve warm.

Mozzarella & Eggplant Lasagna

Servings: 2

Cooking Time: 30 Minutes

Ingredients:

- 1 large eggplant, chopped
- 4 oz mozzarella, chopped
- 3 oz mascarpone cheese
- 2 tomatoes, sliced
- ¼ cup olive oil
- Salt and pepper to taste

Directions:

1. Grease a baking dish with olive oil. Slice the eggplant and make a layer in the dish. Cover with mozzarella and tomato slices. Top with mascarpone cheese. Repeat the process until you run out of ingredients.
2. In a bowl, mix olive oil, salt, and pepper. Pour the mixture over the lasagna, and add ½ cup of water. In your pot, pour 1 cup of water and insert a trivet. Lower the baking dish on the trivet, seal the lid and cook on High Pressure for 4 minutes. Do a natural release for 10 minutes.

Stuffed Potatoes With Feta & Rosemary

Servings: 4

Cooking Time: 50 Minutes

Ingredients:

- 1 cup button mushrooms, chopped
- 6 whole potatoes
- ¼ cup olive oil
- 3 garlic cloves, minced
- ¼ cup feta cheese
- 1 tsp rosemary, chopped
- ½ tsp dried thyme
- 1 tsp salt

Directions:

1. Rub the potatoes with salt and place them in the Instant Pot. Add enough water to cover and seal the lid. Cook on High Pressure for 30 minutes. Do a quick release and remove the potatoes. Let chill for a while.
2. In the pot, mix oil, garlic, rosemary, thyme, and mushrooms. Sauté until the mushrooms soften, 5 minutes on Sauté. Stir in feta. Cut the top of each potato and spoon out the middle. Fill with cheese mixture and serve.

Quick Cassoulet

Servings:6

Cooking Time: 45 Minutes

Ingredients:

- 1 tablespoon olive oil
- 1 medium yellow onion, peeled and diced
- 2 cups dried cannellini beans, rinsed and drained
- 2 medium carrots, peeled and diced small
- 1 tablespoon Italian seasoning
- 1 teaspoon garlic salt
- ½ teaspoon ground black pepper
- 2 ½ cups vegetable broth
- 1 can diced tomatoes, including juice
- 4 vegan smoked apple sausages, each cut into 4 sections

Directions:

1. Press the Sauté button on the Instant Pot and heat oil. Add onion and stir-fry 3–5 minutes until onions are translucent. Add beans and toss.
2. Add carrots, Italian seasoning, garlic salt, and pepper.
3. Gently pour in broth and diced tomatoes. Press the Cancel button. Lock lid.
4. Press the Bean button and cook for the default time of 30 minutes. When timer beeps, let pressure release naturally for 10 minutes. Quick-release any additional pressure until float valve drops. Press the Cancel button. Unlock lid. Add sausage.
5. Press the Sauté button on the Instant Pot, press the Adjust button to change the temperature to Less, and simmer bean mixture unlidded 10 minutes to thicken. Transfer to a serving bowl and carefully toss. Serve warm.

Sweet Potato Medallions With Garlic

Servings: 4

Cooking Time: 25 Minutes

Ingredients:

- 1 tbsp fresh rosemary
- 1 tbsp garlic powder
- 4 sweet potatoes
- 2 tbsp butter
- Salt to taste

Directions:

1. Add 1 cup water and place a steamer rack over the water. Use a fork to prick sweet potatoes all over and set onto the steamer rack. Seal the lid and cook on High Pressure for 12 minutes. Release the pressure quickly. Transfer sweet potatoes to a cutting board. Peel and slice them into ½-inch medallions. Melt butter in the on Sauté. Add in the medallions and cook each side for 2 to 3 minutes until browned. Season with salt and garlic powder. Serve topped with rosemary.

Sautéed Spinach With Roquefort Cheese

Servings: 2

Cooking Time: 10 Minutes

Ingredients:

- ½ cup Roquefort cheese, crumbled
- 9 oz fresh spinach
- 2 leeks, chopped
- 2 red onions, chopped
- 2 garlic cloves, crushed
- 3 tbsp olive oil

Directions:

1. Grease the inner pot with oil. Stir-fry leeks, garlic, and onions for about 5 minutes on Sauté. Add spinach and give it a good stir. Press Cancel, transfer to a serving dish, and sprinkle with Roquefort cheese. Serve right away.

Black Bean Slider Patties

Servings:8

Cooking Time: 49 Minutes

Ingredients:

- 1 tablespoon olive oil
- 1 small red bell pepper, seeded and diced small
- 2 cups vegetable broth
- 1 cup dried black beans, rinsed and drained
- 2 teaspoons chili powder
- ½ teaspoon salt
- ½ teaspoon ground black pepper
- 1 large egg
- 1 cup panko bread crumbs

Directions:

1. Press the Sauté button on the Instant Pot and heat oil. Add bell pepper and stir-fry 2–3 minutes until pepper is tender. Add broth and deglaze by scraping the bottom and sides of pot.
2. Add beans, chili powder, salt, and pepper. Press the Cancel button. Lock lid.
3. Press the Bean button and cook for the default time of 30 minutes. When timer beeps, let pressure release naturally for 10 minutes. Quick-release any additional pressure until float valve drops. Press the Cancel button. Unlock lid.
4. Press the Sauté button on the Instant Pot, press the Adjust button to change the heat to Less, and simmer bean mixture unlidded 10 minutes to thicken. Transfer mixture to a large bowl.
5. Once bean mixture is cool enough to handle, quickly mix in egg and bread crumbs. Form into sixteen equal-sized small patties.
6. In a medium skillet over medium heat, cook patties approximately 2–3 minutes per side until browned. Serve warm.

Thyme Asparagus Soup

Servings: 4

Cooking Time: 15 Minutes

Ingredients:

- 1 carrot, chopped
- 2 cups sour cream
- ½ lb Asparagus, chopped
- 1 sliced Onion
- 3 Garlic cloves, minced
- 3 tbsp Coconut oil
- ½ tsp dried Thyme
- 5 cups Bone broth
- 1 Lemon, juiced, zested

Directions:

1. Melt coconut oil in your Instant Pot on Sauté. Place the onions and garlic and cook for 2 minutes, stirring often. Add in thyme and cook for 1 minute. Put in bone broth, asparagus, carrot, and lemon zest and seal the lid. Select Manual and cook for 5 minutes on High pressure. When done, perform a quick pressure release and unlock the lid. Mix in sour cream and serve.

Red Wine And Mushroom Risotto

Servings:4

Cooking Time: 19 Minutes

Ingredients:

- 2 tablespoons olive oil
- 1 small yellow onion, peeled and finely diced
- 1 cup sliced baby bella mushrooms
- 2 cloves garlic, peeled and minced
- 1 ½ cups Arborio rice
- 3 cups vegetable broth, divided
- 1 cup dry red wine (cabernet sauvignon or pinot noir)
- ½ teaspoon salt
- ¼ teaspoon ground black pepper

Directions:

1. Press the Sauté button on the Instant Pot and heat oil. Add onion and mushrooms and stir-fry 3–5 minutes until onions are translucent. Add garlic and rice and cook an additional 1 minute. Add 1 cup broth and stir 2–3 minutes until it is absorbed by rice.
2. Add remaining 2 cups broth, wine, salt, and pepper. Press the Cancel button. Lock lid.
3. Press the Manual or Pressure Cook button and adjust time to 10 minutes. When timer beeps, let pressure release naturally for 10 minutes. Quick-release any additional pressure until float valve drops. Unlock lid.
4. Ladle into bowls. Serve warm.

Plant-based Indian Curry

Servings: 4

Cooking Time: 20 Minutes

Ingredients:

- 1 tsp butter
- 1 onion, chopped
- 2 cloves garlic, minced
- 1 tsp ginger, grated
- 1 tsp ground cumin
- 1 tsp red chili powder
- 1 tsp salt
- ½ tsp ground turmeric
- 1 can chickpeas
- 1 tomato, diced
- 1/3 cup water
- 2 lb collard greens, chopped
- ½ tsp garam masala
- 1 tsp lemon juice

Directions:

1. Melt butter on Sauté. Add in the onion, ginger, cumin, turmeric, red chili powder, garlic, and salt and cook for 30 seconds until crispy. Stir in tomato. Pour in ⅓ cup of water and chickpeas. Seal the lid and cook on High Pressure for 4 minutes. Release the pressure quickly. Press Sauté. Into the chickpea mixture, stir in lemon juice, collard greens, and garam masala until well coated. Cook for 2 to 3 minutes until collard greens wilt on Sauté. Serve over rice or naan.

Mashed Potato Balls With Tomato Sauce

Servings: 4

Cooking Time: 55 Minutes

Ingredients:

- 2 potatoes, peeled
- 1 onion, peeled, chopped
- 1 lb spinach, torn
- ¼ cup mozzarella, shredded
- 2 eggs, beaten
- Salt and pepper to taste
- 1 tsp dried oregano
- 1 cup whole milk
- ¼ cup flour
- ¼ cup cornflour
- 2 garlic cloves
- Tomato sauce:
- 1 lb tomatoes, chopped
- 1 onion, chopped
- 2 garlic cloves, minced
- 3 tsp olive oil
- ¼ cup white wine
- 1 tsp sugar
- 1 tsp dried rosemary
- ½ tsp salt
- 1 tsp tomato paste

Directions:

1. Place the potatoes in your Instant Pot and add enough water to cover. Seal the lid and cook on High Pressure for 13 minutes. Do a quick release. Add 1 cup of milk and mash with a potato masher. Whisk in eggs, add onion, spinach, mozzarella, salt, pepper, oregano, flour, cornflour, and garlic, and mix with hands. Shape into balls and set aside. Press Sauté, warm olive oil, and stir-fry onion and garlic until translucent.
2. Stir in tomatoes and cook until tender, about 10 minutes. Pour in the wine and add sugar, rosemary, and salt. Stir in 1 tsp of tomato paste and mix well. Cook for five more minutes. Place the potato balls in the cooker and seal with the lid. Cook on High Pressure for 5 minutes. Do a natural release for 10 minutes. Ser

Parsley Lentil Soup With Vegetables

Servings: 4

Cooking Time: 20 Minutes

Ingredients:

- 1 tbsp olive oil
- 1 onion, chopped
- 1 cup celery, chopped
- 2 garlic cloves, chopped
- 3 cups vegetable stock
- 1 ½ cups lentils, rinsed
- 4 carrots, halved lengthwise
- ½ tsp salt
- 2 tbsp parsley, chopped

Directions:

1. Warm olive oil on Sauté. Add in onion, garlic, and celery and sauté for 5 minutes until soft. Mix in lentils, carrots, salt, and stock. Seal the lid and cook on High Pressure for 10 minutes. Release the pressure quickly. Serve topped with parsley.

Simple Cheese Spinach Dip

Servings: 6

Cooking Time: 20 Minutes

Ingredients:

- 2 cups cream cheese
- 1 cup baby spinach
- 1 cup mozzarella, grated
- Salt and pepper to taste
- ½ cup scallions
- 1 cup vegetable broth

Directions:

1. Place cream cheese, spinach, mozzarella cheese, salt, pepper, scallions, and broth in a mixing bowl. Stir well and transfer to your Instant Pot. Seal the lid and cook on High Pressure for 5 minutes. Release the steam naturally for 10 minutes. Serve with celery sticks or chips.

Vegetarian Green Dip

Servings: 4

Cooking Time: 15 Minutes

Ingredients:

- 10 oz canned green chiles, drained, liquid reserved
- 2 cups broccoli florets
- 1 green bell pepper, diced
- ¼ cup raw cashews
- ¼ cup soy sauce
- ½ tsp sea salt
- ¼ tsp chili powder
- ¼ tsp garlic powder
- ¼ tsp cumin

Directions:

1. In the pot, add cashews, broccoli, green bell pepper, and 1 cup water. Seal the lid and cook for 5 minutes on High Pressure. Release the pressure quickly. Carefully unlock the lid. Drain water from the pot. Add reserved liquid from canned green chiles, salt, garlic powder, chili powder, soy sauce, and cumin. Use an immersion blender to blitz the mixture until smooth. Stir in chiles and serve.

Indian Dhal With Veggies

Servings: 4

Cooking Time: 35 Minutes

Ingredients:

- 1 cup lentils
- 2 tbsp almond butter
- 1 carrot, peeled, chopped
- 1 potato, peeled, chopped
- 1 bay leaf
- ¼ tbsp parsley, chopped
- ½ tbsp chili powder
- 2 tbsp ground cumin
- 1 tbsp garam masala
- 3 cups vegetable stock

Directions:

1. Melt almond butter on Sauté. Add carrots, pota-

toes, and bay leaf. Stir and cook for 10 minutes. Add lentils, chili powder, cumin, garam masala, and stock and press Cancel. If the mixture is very thick, add a bit of water. Seal the lid, select Manual, and cook on High Pressure for 15 minutes. Once the timer goes off, do a quick release. Serve sprinkled with parsley.

Wheat Berry Salad

Servings:6

Cooking Time: 35 Minutes

Ingredients:

- 3 tablespoons olive oil, divided
- 1 cup wheat berries
- 2¼ cups water, divided
- 2 cups peeled and shredded carrots
- 2 apples, peeled, cored, and diced small
- ½ cup raisins
- 2 tablespoons pure maple syrup
- 2 teaspoons orange zest
- ¼ cup fresh orange juice
- 1 tablespoon balsamic vinegar
- ½ teaspoon salt

Directions:

1. Press Sauté button on Instant Pot. Heat 1 tablespoon oil and add wheat berries. Stir-fry for 4–5 minutes until browned and fragrant. Add 2 cups water. Lock lid.
2. Press the Manual button and adjust time to 30 minutes. When timer beeps, let pressure release naturally for 10 minutes. Quick-release any additional pressure until float valve drops and then unlock lid.
3. Let cool for 10 minutes and drain any additional liquid.
4. Transfer cooled berries to a medium bowl and add remaining ingredients. Refrigerate covered overnight until ready to serve chilled.

Curly Kale Soup

Servings: 4

Cooking Time: 20 Minutes

Ingredients:

- 4 cups curly kale
- 2 tbsp Ginger, minced
- 4 Garlic cloves, minced
- 1 tbsp Mustard seeds
- 1 tbsp Olive oil
- 1 cup Heavy cream
- 2 cups vegetable broth
- 1 tbsp Cumin powder

Directions:

1. Warm olive oil in your Instant Pot on Sauté. Place the mustard seeds, garlic, ginger, cumin powder, vegetable broth, curly kale, and heavy cream. Seal the lid, select Manual, and cook for 10 minutes on High pressure. When done, perform a quick pressure release and unlock the lid. Serve warm.

Cauliflower & Potato Curry With Cilantro

Servings: 4

Cooking Time: 40 Minutes

Ingredients:

- 1 tbsp vegetable oil
- 10 oz cauliflower florets
- 1 potato, peeled and diced
- 1 tbsp ghee
- 2 tbsp cumin seeds
- 1 onion, minced
- 4 garlic cloves, minced
- 1 tomato, chopped
- 1 jalapeño pepper, minced
- 1 tbsp curry paste
- 1 tbsp ground turmeric
- ½ tsp chili pepper
- Salt and pepper to taste
- 2 tbsp cilantro, chopped

Directions:

1. Warm oil on Sauté. Add in potato and cauliflower and cook for 8 to 10 minutes until lightly browned; season with salt. Set the vegetables in a bowl. Add ghee to the pot. Mix in cumin seeds and cook for 10 seconds until they start to pop; add onion and cook for 3 minutes until softened. Mix in garlic and pepper; cook for 30 seconds.
2. Add in tomato, curry paste, chili pepper, jalapeño pepper, and turmeric; cook for 4 to 6 minutes. Return potato and cauliflower to the pot. Stir in 1 cup water. Seal the lid and cook on High Pressure for 4 minutes. Quick-release the pressure. Unlock the lid. Top with cilantro and serve.

Vegetarian Chili With Lentils & Quinoa

Servings: 4

Cooking Time: 45 Minutes

Ingredients:

- 28-oz can diced tomatoes
- 1 cups cashew, chopped
- 1 cup onion, chopped
- ½ cup red lentils
- ½ cup red quinoa
- 2 chipotle peppers, minced
- 2 garlic cloves, minced
- 1 tsp chili powder
- 1 tsp salt
- 1 cup carrots, chopped
- 1 can black beans
- ¼ cup parsley, chopped

Directions:

1. In the pot, mix tomatoes, onion, chipotle peppers, chili powder, lentils, cashew, carrot, quinoa, garlic, and salt. Cover with water. Seal the lid, Press Soup/Stew, and cook for 30 minutes on High Pressure. Release the pressure quickly. Add in black beans. Simmer on Sauté until heated through. Top with parsley and serve.

Quinoa Endive Boats

Servings: 4

Cooking Time: 3 Minutes

Ingredients:

- 1 tablespoon walnut oil
- 1 cup quinoa
- 2½ cups water
- 2 cups chopped jarred artichoke hearts
- 2 cups diced tomatoes, seeded
- ½ small red onion, peeled and thinly sliced
- 2 tablespoons olive oil
- 1 tablespoon balsamic vinegar
- 2 heads Belgian endive
- 1 cup roasted pecans

Directions:

1. Press the Sauté button on Instant Pot. Heat walnut oil. Add quinoa and toss for 1 minute until slightly browned. Add water. Lock lid.
2. Press the Manual button and adjust time to 2 minutes. When timer beeps, let pressure release naturally for 10 minutes. Quick-release any additional pressure until float valve drops and then unlock lid. Drain liquid and transfer quinoa to a serving bowl.
3. Toss remaining ingredients except endive leaves and pecans into quinoa. Refrigerate mixture covered until cooled for 1 hour up to overnight.
4. To prepare boats, separate the endive leaves. Rinse, drain, and divide them among four plates. Top each with ¼ of the quinoa mixture. Distribute ¼ cup toasted pecans over the top of each endive boat and serve.

Coconut Milk Yogurt With Honey

Servings: 6

Cooking Time: 15 Hours

Ingredients:

- 2 cans coconut milk
- 1 tbsp gelatin
- 1 tbsp honey
- 1 tbsp probiotic powder
- Zest from 1 lime

Directions:

1. Into the pot, stir in gelatin and coconut milk until well dissolved. Seal the lid, Press Yogurt until the display is reading "Boil". Once done, the screen will then display "Yogurt". Ensure milk temperature is at 180°F. Remove steel pot from Pressure cooker base and place into a large ice bath to cool milk for 5 minutes to reach 112°F.
2. Remove the pot from the ice bath and wipe the outside dry. Into the coconut milk mixture, add probiotic powder, honey, and Lime zest, and stir to combine. Return steel pot to the base of the Instant Pot. Seal the lid, press Yogurt, and cook for 10 hours. Once complete, spoon yogurt into glass jars with rings and lids; place in the refrigerator to chill for 4 hours to thicken.

Cannellini Beans With Garlic & Leeks

Servings: 4

Cooking Time: 45 Minutes

Ingredients:

- 1 lb cannellini beans
- 1 onion, chopped
- 2 large leeks, finely chopped
- 3 garlic cloves, whole
- Salt and pepper to taste
- Topping
- 2 tbsp vegetable oil
- 2 tbsp flour
- 1 tbsp cayenne pepper

Directions:

1. Add beans, onion, leeks, garlic, salt, and pepper to the Instant Pot. Press Manual/Pressure Cook and cook for 20 minutes on High. Heat the vegetable oil in a skillet. Add flour and cayenne pepper. Stir-fry for 2 minutes and set aside. When done, do a quick release. Pour in the cayenne mixture and give it a good stir. Let it sit for 15 minutes before serving.

Zucchini Pomodoro

Servings:4

Cooking Time: 12 Minutes

Ingredients:

- 1 tablespoon avocado oil
- 1 large onion, peeled and diced
- 3 cloves garlic, minced
- 1 can diced tomatoes, including juice
- ½ cup water
- 1 tablespoon Italian seasoning
- 1 teaspoon sea salt
- ½ teaspoon ground black pepper
- 2 medium zucchini, spiraled

Directions:

1. Press Sauté button on the Instant Pot. Heat avocado oil. Add onions and stir-fry for 3–5 minutes until translucent. Add garlic and cook for an additional minute. Add tomatoes, water, Italian seasoning, salt, and pepper. Add zucchini and toss to combine. Lock lid.
2. Press the Manual button and adjust time to 1 minute. When timer beeps, let pressure release naturally for 5 minutes. Quick-release any additional pressure until float valve drops and then unlock lid.
3. Transfer zucchini to four bowls. Press Sauté button, press Adjust button to change the temperature to Less, and simmer sauce in the Instant Pot unlidded for 5 minutes. Ladle over zucchini and serve immediately.

Mighty "meat"loaf

Servings:4

Cooking Time: 12 Minutes

Ingredients:

- 1 can cannellini beans, drained and rinsed
- 1 cup finely chopped baby bella mushrooms
- 2 small shallots, minced
- 1 large carrot, peeled and grated
- 2 garlic cloves, minced
- 2 large eggs, whisked

- 1 cup shredded mozzarella cheese
- 1 tablespoon Italian seasoning
- 1 teaspoon sea salt
- ½ teaspoon ground black pepper
- 1 cup old-fashioned oats
- 1 tablespoon Dijon mustard
- 1 can tomato sauce
- 1 cup water

Directions:

1. Add beans to a medium mixing bowl. Using the back of a wooden spoon, smash the beans against the side of the bowl until they all pop open. Add remaining ingredients except water and mix well. Form mixture into a ball and place into a greased 7-cup glass bowl. Slightly press down the top of the ball.
2. Pour 1 cup water into Instant Pot. Insert trivet. Place glass bowl onto trivet. Lock lid.
3. Press the Manual button and adjust time to 12 minutes. When timer beeps, quick-release pressure until float valve drops and then unlock lid. Remove bowl from Instant Pot and let cool for 15 minutes before serving.

Basil Parmesan Sauce

Servings: 4

Cooking Time: 10 Minutes

Ingredients:

- 1 cup fresh basil, torn
- 1 cup cream cheese
- 2 tbsp Parmesan, shredded
- 1 tbsp olive oil
- Salt and pepper to taste
- 2 cups vegetable broth

Directions:

1. In the Instant Pot, stir basil, cream cheese, Parmesan, oil, salt, pepper, and broth. Seal the lid and cook on High Pressure for 5 minutes. Do a quick pressure release and unlock the lid. Serve immediately.

Creamy Turnips Stuffed With Cheese

Servings: 4

Cooking Time: 20 Minutes

Ingredients:

- ½ cup chopped roasted red bell pepper
- 4 small turnips
- ¼ cup whipping cream
- ¼ cup sour cream
- 1 tsp Italian seasoning
- 1 ½ cups grated mozzarella
- 4 green onions, chopped
- 1/3 cup grated Parmesan

Directions:

1. Pour 1 cup of water into the pot and insert a trivet. Place the turnips on top. Seal the lid and cook on High for 10 minutes. Do a quick pressure release. Remove the turnips to a cutting board and allow cooling. Cut the turnips in half. Scoop out the pulp into a bowl and mash it with a potato mash. Mix in the whipping and sour cream until smooth. Stir in the roasted bell pepper.
2. Add in Italian seasoning and mozzarella cheese. Fetch out 2 tbsp of green onions and put into the turnips. Fill the turnip skins with the mashed mixture and sprinkle with Parmesan cheese. Arrange on a greased baking dish and place on the trivet. Seal the lid and cook on High pressure for 3 minutes. Do a quick pressure release. Top with the remaining onions to serve.

English Vegetable Potage

Servings: 4

Cooking Time: 50 Minutes

Ingredients:

- 1 lb potatoes, cut into bite-sized pieces
- 2 carrots, peeled, chopped
- 3 celery stalks, chopped
- 2 onions, peeled, chopped
- 1 zucchini, sliced
- A handful of celery leaves
- 2 tbsp butter, unsalted
- 3 tbsp olive oil
- 2 cups vegetable broth
- 1 tbsp paprika
- Salt and pepper to taste
- 2 bay leaves

Directions:

1. Warm olive oil on Sauté and stir-fry the onions for 3-4 minutes until translucent. Add carrots, celery, zucchini, and ¼ cup of broth. Continue to cook for 10 more minutes, stirring constantly. Stir in potatoes, paprika, salt, pepper, bay leaves, remaining broth, and celery leaves. Seal the lid and cook on Meat/Stew for 30 minutes on High. Do a quick release and stir in butter.

Stuffed Avocado Bake

Servings: 2

Cooking Time: 20 Minutes

Ingredients:

- 1 avocado, halved
- 2 eggs
- 3 tbsp butter, melted
- 1 tbsp dried oregano
- Salt and pepper to taste
- 1 tomato, chopped

Directions:

1. Grease a baking dish with butter. With a spoon, remove some of the avocado flesh to create more space for the eggs. Reserve the flesh for garnish. Place the avocado in the baking dish. Crack an egg into each avocado half. Season with salt and oregano. Add 1 cup of water and place the trivet in the pot. Lower the baking dish on top.
2. Seal the lid, select Manual, and cook on High Pressure for 10 minutes. When done, do a quick release before opening the lid. Mix the reserved avocado flesh with the tomato, season with salt and pepper and serve with the baked avocado.

Pork, Beef & Lamb

Pork, Beef & Lamb

Easy Ground Bulgogi

Servings:4

Cooking Time: 5 Minutes

Ingredients:

- 1 tablespoon olive oil
- 1 pound 80/20 ground beef
- 3 medium green onions, sliced (whites and greens separated)
- 3 cloves garlic, peeled and minced
- ¼ cup soy sauce
- ¼ cup granulated sugar
- 2 teaspoons hot sauce
- 1 teaspoon minced ginger

Directions:

1. Press the Sauté button on the Instant Pot and heat oil. Add ground beef and onion whites. Stir-fry 3–4 minutes until onions are tender and beef is almost all brown. Add garlic and heat 1 additional minute.
2. Stir in soy sauce, sugar, hot sauce, and ginger. Press the Cancel button. Lock lid.
3. Press the Manual or Pressure Cook button and adjust time to 0 minutes. When timer beeps, quick-release pressure until float valve drops. Unlock lid.
4. Transfer pot ingredients to bowls. Garnish with onion greens. Serve warm.

Tasty Beef Cutlets With Vegetables

Servings: 4

Cooking Time: 45 Minutes

Ingredients:

- 2 large beef cutlets
- 4 whole potatoes, peeled
- 1 whole onion, peeled

- 1 whole carrot, peeled
- 10 oz cauliflower florets
- 3 tbsp olive oil
- 1 tbsp butter
- Salt and pepper to taste
- 3 cups beef broth

Directions:

1. Sprinkle the meat with salt and pepper and place it in your Instant Pot. Add in cauliflower, onion, carrot, and potatoes. Pour in broth, seal the lid, and cook on High Pressure for 25 minutes. Release the pressure naturally for about 10 minutes. Remove the meat and vegetables. Melt butter and oil on Sauté. Add the meat. Brown on both sides and serve with vegetables.

Thyme Beef With Mushrooms & Tomatoes

Servings: 4

Cooking Time: 30 Minutes

Ingredients:

- 1 lb button mushrooms, chopped
- 1 lb beef steaks
- 2 tbsp vegetable oil
- Salt and pepper to taste
- 1 tbsp dried thyme
- 6 oz cherry tomatoes

Directions:

1. Rub steaks with salt, pepper, and thyme. Place in the Instant Pot. Pour in 3 cups of water and seal the lid. Cook on High Pressure for 13 minutes. Do a quick release and set the steaks aside. Heat oil on Sauté, and stir-fry mushrooms and tomatoes for 5 minutes. Add steaks and brown on both sides. Serve.

Korean Short Ribs

Servings:6

Cooking Time: 25 Minutes

Ingredients:

- ½ cup soy sauce
- ½ cup pure maple syrup
- ½ cup rice wine
- 1 tablespoon sesame oil
- 1 teaspoon white pepper
- ½ teaspoon ground ginger
- ½ teaspoon garlic powder
- ½ teaspoon gochujang
- 3 pounds beef short ribs
- 1 cup beef broth
- 2 green onions, sliced
- 1 tablespoon toasted sesame seeds

Directions:

1. In a small bowl, combine soy sauce, maple syrup, rice wine, sesame oil, white pepper, ground ginger, garlic powder, and gochujang. Using your hands, rub this mixture into the rib sections. Refrigerate covered for 60 minutes up to overnight.
2. Add beef broth to Instant Pot. Insert trivet. Arrange ribs standing upright with the meaty side facing outward. Lock lid.
3. Press the Manual button and adjust time to 25 minutes. When the timer beeps, let pressure release naturally until float valve drops and then unlock lid.
4. Transfer ribs to a serving platter and garnish with green onions and sesame seeds.

Beer-braised Pork

Servings: 4

Cooking Time: 53 Minutes

Ingredients:

- 2 lb pork loin roast
- 2 tbsp butter
- 1 onion, chopped
- 2 garlic cloves, minced
- 1 tsp thyme
- 1 bay leaf
- 2 cups beer
- Salt and pepper to taste

Directions:

1. Melt butter in your Instant Pot on Sauté. Place the pork roast fatty-side down and cook on both sides. Add in onion and garlic and cook for 3 minutes. Put in thyme, salt, pepper, beer, bay leaf, and ½ cup of water and seal the lid. Select Manual and cook for 30 minutes on High.
2. When over, allow a natural release for 10 minutes and unlock the lid. Transfer roast to a bowl and cover it. Press Sauté and cook until the sauce thickens. Cut the roast and top with the sauce.

Red Wine Beef & Vegetable Hotpot

Servings: 6

Cooking Time: 40 Minutes

Ingredients:

- 2 sweet potatoes, cut into chunks
- 2 lb stewing beef meat
- ¾ cup red wine
- 1 tbsp ghee
- 6 oz tomato paste
- 6 oz baby carrots, chopped
- 1 onion, finely chopped
- ½ tsp salt
- 4 cups beef broth
- ½ cup green peas
- 1 tsp dried thyme
- 3 garlic cloves, crushed

Directions:

1. Heat ghee on Sauté. Add beef and brown for 5-6 minutes. Add onion and garlic, and keep stirring for 3 more minutes. Add the sweet potatoes, wine, tomato paste, carrots, salt, broth, green peas, and thyme and seal the lid. Cook on Meat/Stew for 20 minutes on High Pressure. Do a quick release. Serve.

Delicious Pork & Vegetables Soup

Servings: 4

Cooking Time: 50 Minutes

Ingredients:

- 2 pork chops
- 1 tbsp cayenne pepper
- 1 tsp chili powder
- ½ tsp garlic powder
- 4 cups beef broth
- 2 tbsp olive oil
- 2 large carrots, chopped
- 2 celery stalks, diced
- 1 onion, diced
- 2 tbsp soy sauce

Directions:

1. Warm the olive oil in your Instant Pot on Sauté and stir-fry the onion until translucent, 3 minutes. Add celery stalks, carrots, cayenne, and chili pepper. Give it a good stir and continue to cook for 6-7 minutes. Add in pork chops, garlic, and soy sauce.
2. Pour in the broth and seal the lid. Cook on Manual for 25 minutes on High. Do a quick release. Let chill for 5 minutes. Serve.

Steak Fajitas

Servings: 6

Cooking Time: 45 Minutes

Ingredients:

- ⅛ cup avocado oil
- ¼ cup coconut aminos
- 1 tablespoon fish sauce
- 1 teaspoon ground cumin
- 1 teaspoon chili powder
- 2 tablespoons tomato paste
- ½ teaspoon sea salt
- 1 skirt steak
- 1 small onion, peeled and diced
- 1 medium green bell pepper, seeded and diced
- 1 medium red bell pepper, seeded and diced
- 1 cup beef broth

Directions:

1. In a small bowl, combine oil, coconut aminos, fish sauce, cumin, chili powder, tomato paste, and salt. Spread ¾ of the mixture on all sides of the beef. Reserve additional sauce.
2. Press the Sauté button on Instant Pot. Add skirt steak and sear on each side for approximately 5 minutes. Remove the meat and set aside. Add onion and peppers to Instant Pot with reserved sauce. Sauté for 3–5 minutes until onions are translucent.
3. Add beef broth. Set meat on the layer of onion and peppers. Lock lid.
4. Press the Meat button and cook for the default time of 35 minutes. When timer beeps, let the pressure release naturally until float valve drops and then unlock lid.
5. Using a slotted spoon, remove the meat and vegetables to a serving platter. Thinly slice the skirt steak against the grain. Serve.

Creamy Beef & Cauliflower Chili

Servings: 6

Cooking Time: 20 Minutes

Ingredients:

- 1 lb beef stew meat
- 4 oz cauliflower, chopped
- 1 onion, chopped
- 2 cups beef broth
- 2 cups heavy cream
- 1 tsp Italian seasoning
- 1 tsp salt
- ½ tsp chili pepper

Directions:

1. Add beef, cauliflower, onion, broth, heavy cream, Italian seasoning, salt, and chili pepper to your Instant Pot. Pour in 1 cup water. Seal the lid and cook on High Pressure for 15 minutes. When ready, do a quick release and serve.

Fennel Pork Butt With Mushrooms

Servings: 8

Cooking Time: 30 Minutes

Ingredients:

- 1 lb pork butt, sliced
- 2 cups mushrooms, sliced
- 1 fennel bulb, chopped
- ½ cup white wine
- ½ cup vegetable broth
- Salt and pepper to taste

Directions:

1. Grease with cooking spray and heat on Sauté. Brown the pork slices and for a few minutes. Stir in mushrooms, fennel, wine, broth, salt, and pepper. Seal the lid and cook for 20 minutes on Meat/Stew on High. When done, do a quick release.

Vietnamese Beef

Servings: 6

Cooking Time: 60 Minutes

Ingredients:

- 2 lb beef steak, sliced
- 3 tbsp olive oil
- Salt and pepper to taste
- 4 garlic cloves, minced
- 1 tsp minced ginger
- 3 white onions, chopped
- 3 tbsp fish sauce
- 1 tbsp brown sugar
- 2 tbsp cornflour
- 2 tbsp mint leaves, chopped
- 1 red chili pepper, minced

Directions:

1. Sprinkle beef steak with salt and pepper. Warm the olive oil in your Instant Pot on Sauté. Place in the steak and sauté for 10-12 minutes on all sides. Set aside.
2. Add garlic, ginger, red chili pepper, and onions to the pot and cook for 2-3 minutes. Stir in fish sauce, brown sugar, and 1 ¼ cups of water. Put the steak back to the pot.
3. Seal the lid. Select Manual and cook for 25 minutes on High pressure. When done, allow a natural release for 10 minutes, then perform a quick pressure release, and unlock the lid. Combine ½ cup of water and cornflour in a bowl and pour it into the pot. Simmer on Sauté until the liquid thickens. Serve topped with mint leaves.

Paprika Pork Fajitas With Cotija Cheese

Servings: 4

Cooking Time: 1 Hour 30 Minutes

Ingredients:

- ½ cup queso Cotija, crumbled
- 1 tbsp ground cumin
- 2 tsp dried oregano
- 1 tsp paprika
- 1 tsp onion powder
- Salt and pepper to taste
- ½ tsp ground cinnamon
- 2 lb boneless pork shoulder
- ¾ cup vegetable broth
- ¼ cup pineapple juice
- 1 lime, juiced
- 4 cloves garlic, crushed
- 2 bay leaves
- 4 corn tortillas, warmed

Directions:

1. In a bowl, combine cumin, paprika, pepper, onion powder, oregano, salt, and cinnamon; toss in pork to coat. Place the pork, broth, garlic, lime juice, bay leaves, and pineapple juice in the Instant Pot. Seal the lid. Cook on High Pressure for 50 minutes. Release pressure quickly. Transfer the pork to a baking sheet and shred it with 2 forks. Reserve juices in the pot.
2. Preheat oven to 450 F. Bake in the oven for 10 minutes until crispy. Skim and get rid of fat from the liquid remaining in the pot. Dispose of the bay leaves. Over the pork, pour the liquid and serve alongside warm corn tortillas and queso Cotija.

Beef Arancini With Potatoes

Servings: 4

Cooking Time: 40 Minutes

Ingredients:

- 1 lb lean ground beef
- 6 oz rice
- 2 onions, peeled, chopped
- 2 garlic cloves, crushed
- 1 egg, beaten
- 1 potato peeled, chopped
- 3 tbsp olive oil
- 1 tsp salt

Directions:

1. In a bowl, combine beef, rice, onions, garlic, egg, and salt. Shape the mixture into 15-16 meatballs. Grease the inner pot with 1 tbsp of olive oil. Press Sauté and cook the meatballs for 3-4 minutes, or until slightly brown.
2. Remove the meatballs. Add the remaining oil and make a layer of potato. Top with meatballs, cover with water, and seal the lid. Adjust the release steam handle. Cook on Meat/Stew for 15 minutes on High. Do a quick release.

Balsamic Pork Chops With Figs And Pears

Servings:2

Cooking Time: 15 Minutes

Ingredients:

- 2 bone-in pork chops
- 1 teaspoon sea salt
- 1 teaspoon ground black pepper
- ¼ cup balsamic vinegar
- ¼ cup chicken broth
- 1 tablespoon dried mint
- 2 tablespoons avocado oil
- 1 medium sweet onion, peeled and sliced
- 3 pears, peeled, cored, and diced large
- 5 dried figs, stems removed and halved

Directions:

1. Pat the pork chops dry with a paper towel and season both sides liberally with salt and pepper. Set aside.
2. In a small bowl, whisk together vinegar, broth, and mint. Set aside.
3. Press the Sauté button on the Instant Pot. Heat oil. Brown pork chops for 5 minutes per side. Remove chops and set aside.
4. Add vinegar mixture and deglaze the Instant Pot by scraping the brown bits from the sides and bottom of the Instant Pot. Layer the onions into the pot, then scatter the pears and figs over onions. Place pork chops on top. Lock lid.
5. Press the Steam button and adjust time to 3 minutes. When the timer beeps, let pressure release naturally for 10 minutes. Quick-release any additional pressure until the float valve drops and then unlock lid.
6. Using a slotted spoon, transfer pork, onions, figs, and pears to a serving platter. Serve warm.

Broccoli & Cauliflower Pork Sausages

Servings: 6

Cooking Time: 20 Minutes

Ingredients:

- 1 lb pork sausage, sliced
- ½ lb broccoli florets
- ½ lb cauliflower florets
- 14 oz can mushroom soup
- 10 oz evaporated milk
- Salt and pepper to taste

Directions:

1. Place ¼ of the sausage slices in your pressure cooker. In a bowl, whisk the soup, salt, pepper, and milk. Pour some of the mixtures over the sausages. Top the sausage slices with ¼ of the cauliflower and broccoli florets. Pour some of the soup mixtures again. Repeat the layers until you use up all ingredients. Seal the lid and cook on Pressure Cook for 10 minutes on High. When ready, do a quick release. Serve.

Sambal Beef Noodles

Servings: 4

Cooking Time: 65 Minutes

Ingredients:

- 1 lb beef chuck roast, cubed
- 2 tbsp sesame oil
- Salt and pepper to taste
- 1 chopped onion
- 2 minced garlic cloves
- 3 tbsp sambal oelek chili paste
- 2 cups water
- 8 oz egg noodles

Directions:

1. Warm the sesame oil in your Instant Pot on Sauté. Place in the beef roast and cook for 6-7 minutes, stirring often. Add in salt, pepper, onion, sambal oelek chili paste, garlic, and 1 cup of water. Seal the lid, select Manual, and cook for 30 minutes on High pressure.
2. Once done, allow a natural release for 10 minutes, then perform a quick pressure release. Transfer beef roast to a plate. Pour in 1 cup of water in the pot and bring to a boil on Sauté. Add in noodles and cook for 4-5 minutes. Put the beef back to the pot and stir. Serve warm.

Mexican Pork Chili Verde

Servings: 4

Cooking Time: 45 Minutes

Ingredients:

- 2 lb pork shoulder, cubed
- ½ lb tomatillos, quartered
- 2 serrano peppers, chopped
- 2 jalapeño peppers, minced
- 1 onion, chopped
- 4 garlic cloves, minced
- 1 tsp cayenne pepper
- ½ tsp oregano
- ½ tsp ground coriander
- 1 tsp cumin
- 1 cup chicken stock
- 2 tbsp cilantro, chopped
- Salt and pepper to taste

Directions:

1. Place pork shoulder, tomatillos, serrano peppers, jalapeño peppers, onion, garlic cloves, cayenne pepper, oregano, ground coriander, cumin, chicken stock, salt, and pepper in your Instant Pot and stir. Seal the lid, select Manual, and cook for 35 minutes on High pressure. Once done, perform a quick pressure release and unlock the lid. Transfer the pork to a plate. Put the cilantro in the pot and blend sauce using an immersion blender. Put the pork back in the pot and toss to coat. Serve immediately.

Japanese-style Pork Tenderloin

Servings: 4

Cooking Time: 30 Minutes

Ingredients:

- 2 lb pork tenderloins
- 2 tbsp peanut butter
- 1 cup teriyaki sauce
- ¼ cup coconut milk
- 1 tbsp sesame seeds
- 1 tbsp light soy sauce
- Salt and pepper to taste
- 4 green onions, chopped
- 1 lime, zested

Directions:

1. Melt peanut butter in your Instant Pot on Sauté. Sprinkle pork tenderloins with salt and pepper, place it in the pot and brown for a few minutes on all sides. Put in teriyaki sauce, soy sauce, lime zest, coconut milk, and 1/2 cup of water and seal the lid. Select Manual. Cook for 15 minutes on High.
2. Once done, allow a natural release for 10 minutes, then perform a quick pressure release, and unlock the lid. Slice the tenderloin and garnish with toasted sesame seeds, green onions, and cooking juice. Serve immediately.

Pork Chops With Brussels Sprouts

Servings: 4

Cooking Time: 35 Minutes

Ingredients:

- 1 lb pork chops
- 1 cup onions, sliced
- 1 cup carrots, sliced
- 1 tbsp butter
- 2 cups Brussels sprouts
- 1 tbsp arrowroot
- 1 garlic clove, minced
- 1 cup vegetable stock
- Salt and pepper to taste

Directions:

1. Melt butter on Sauté. Add the pork chops, and cook on all sides until golden in color. Transfer to a plate. Add the onions, and cook for 3 minutes, then add the garlic. Saute for one more minute. Return the pork chops to the pot and pour the stock over. Season with salt and pepper. Seal the lid and cook on High Pressure for 15 minutes.
2. When the timer goes off, do a quick pressure release. Stir in carrots and Brussel sprouts. Seal the lid again and cook for 3 minutes on High Pressure. Do a quick pressure release. Transfer the chops and veggies to a serving platter. Whisk the arrowroot into the pot and cook on Sauté until it thickens. Pour the sauce over the chops and veggies. Serve immediately.

Pulled Pork With Homemade Bbq Sauce

Servings: 6

Cooking Time: 70 Minutes

Ingredients:

- 2 lb pork shoulder
- 1 tbsp onion powder
- 1 tbsp garlic powder
- Salt and pepper to taste
- 1 tbsp chili powder
- 2 cups vegetable stock
- 6 dates, soaked
- ¼ cup tomato paste
- ½ cup coconut aminos

Directions:

1. In a small bowl, combine onion powder, garlic powder, salt, black pepper, and chili powder. Rub the mixture onto the pork. Place the pork inside your pressure cooker. Pour the stock around the meat, not over it, and then seal the lid. Select Pressure Cook and set the timer to 60 minutes. Place the dates, tomato paste, and coconut aminos in a food processor; pulse until smooth. Release the pressure quickly. Grab two forks and shred the meat inside the pot. Pour the sauce over and stir to combine.

Traditional Lamb With Vegetables

Servings: 6

Cooking Time: 30 Minutes

Ingredients:

- 1 lb lamb chops, 1-inch thick
- 1 cup green peas, rinsed
- 3 carrots, chopped
- 3 onions, chopped
- 1 potato, chopped
- 1 tomato, chopped
- 3 tbsp olive oil
- 1 tbsp paprika
- Salt and pepper to taste

Directions:

1. Grease the Instant Pot with olive oil. Rub salt onto the lamb and make a bottom layer. Add peas, carrots, onions, potato, and tomato. Season with paprika. Add olive oil, 1 cup of water, salt, and pepper. Give it a good stir and seal the lid. Cook on Meat/Stew for 20 minutes on High Pressure. When ready, do a natural pressure release. Carefully unlock the lid. Serve hot.

Seasoned Flank Steak

Servings: 8

Cooking Time: 20 Minutes

Ingredients:

- ⅓ cup fresh-squeezed orange juice
- 2 tablespoons honey
- 2 teaspoons ground cumin
- 1 teaspoon salt
- 1 tablespoon sriracha
- 3 tablespoons olive oil, divided
- 2 pounds flank steak
- 1 ½ cups beef broth

Directions:

1. In a small bowl, combine orange juice, honey, cumin, salt, sriracha, and 2 tablespoons oil. Place mixture and flank steak in a large sealable plastic bag. Seal, then massage mixture into meat through the bag. Refrigerate 1 hour.
2. Press the Sauté button on the Instant Pot and heat remaining 1 tablespoon oil. Sear meat on all sides, approximately 4–5 minutes. Add broth to deglaze pot, scraping any bits from the bottom and sides of pot. Press the Cancel button. Lock lid.
3. Press the Manual or Pressure Cook button and adjust time to 15 minutes. When timer beeps, let pressure release naturally for 10 minutes. Quick-release any additional pressure until float valve drops. Unlock lid.
4. Transfer meat to a serving platter. Thinly slice and serve.

Ground Beef & Eggplant Casserole

Servings: 2

Cooking Time: 40 Minutes

Ingredients:

- 2 eggplants, peeled, cut lengthwise
- Salt and pepper to taste
- 1 cup lean ground beef
- 1 onion, chopped
- 1 tsp olive oil
- 2 tomatoes

Directions:

1. Place eggplants in a bowl and season with salt. Let sit for 10 minutes. Rinse well and drain. Grease the inner pot with oil. Stir-fry onion for 2 minutes until soft. Add ground beef, tomatoes, and cook for 5 minutes. Remove to a deep bowl.
2. Make a layer with eggplant slices in the pot. Spread the ground beef mixture over and sprinkle with black pepper and salt. Make another layer with eggplants and repeat until you've used up all ingredients. Seal the lid and cook on High Pressure for 12 minutes. Do a quick release. Serve.

Mushroom Beef Stroganoff

Servings: 6

Cooking Time: 1 Hour

Ingredients:

- ¼ cup flour
- Salt and pepper to taste
- 2 lb beef stew meat
- 2 tbsp olive oil
- 1 onion, chopped
- 2 garlic cloves, minced
- 1 cup beef broth
- 3 cups mushrooms, chopped
- 8 oz sour cream
- 1 tbsp chopped parsley
- 1 cup rice, cooked

Directions:

1. In a large bowl, combine salt, pepper, and flour. Add beef and massage to coat beef in flour mixture. Warm oil on Sauté. Brown the beef for 4 to 5 minutes. Add garlic and onion and cook for 3 minutes until fragrant. Add beef broth to the pot.
2. Seal the lid and cook on High Pressure for 35 minutes. Release the pressure quickly. Open the lid and stir mushrooms and sour cream into the beef mixture. Seal the lid and cook on High Pressure for 2 minutes. Release the pressure quickly. Scoop over cooked rice. Season the stroganoff with pepper, parsley, and salt. Serve warm.

Pork Tenderloin With Balsamic & Butter

Servings: 4

Cooking Time: 50 Minutes

Ingredients:

- 2 lb pork tenderloin
- 2 tbsp butter, unsalted
- 2 tbsp brown sugar
- 2 tbsp balsamic vinegar
- 2 garlic cloves, crushed
- 1 cup beef broth
- Salt and pepper to taste
- 1 tbsp cornstarch

Directions:

1. Melt butter on Sauté in your Instant Pot. Stir-fry garlic for 1 minute. Add in sugar and vinegar and cook for 1 more minute. Rub the meat with salt and pepper. Place it in the pot and pour in the broth. Seal the lid. Cook on High Pressure for 35 minutes. Do a quick release and unlock the lid. Set the meat aside. Stir in cornstarch in the remaining liquid and cook for 1 minute on Sauté to thicken the sauce. Drizzle over meat and serve.

German-style Red Cabbage With Apples

Servings: 4

Cooking Time: 20 Minutes

Ingredients:

- 1 cup Granny Smith apples, cubed
- 1 head red cabbage, shredded
- 2 tbsp olive oil
- 4 oz bacon, chopped
- 1 sweet onion, chopped
- 2 garlic cloves, chopped
- 1 tbsp red wine vinegar
- 1 tsp ground cumin
- Salt and pepper to taste

Directions:

1. Warm olive oil in your Instant Pot on Sauté. Place the bacon, onion, and garlic and cook for 5 minutes.
2. Put in cabbage, vinegar, apples, cumin, salt, pepper, and 1 cup of water and seal the lid. Select Manual and cook for 10 minutes on High pressure. When done, perform a quick pressure release. Carefully unlock the lid. Adjust the taste with salt and pepper and serve.

Butternut Squash & Beef Stew

Servings: 6

Cooking Time: 40 Minutes

Ingredients:

- 2 lb stew beef, cut into 1-inch chunks
- ½ butternut pumpkin, chopped
- 2 tbsp canola oil
- 1 cup red wine
- 1 onion, chopped
- 1 tsp garlic powder
- 1 tsp salt
- 3 whole cloves
- 1 bay leaf
- 3 carrots, chopped
- 2 tbsp cornstarch
- 3 tbsp water

Directions:

1. Warm oil on Sauté. Brown the beef for 5 minutes on each side. Deglaze the pot with wine, scrape the bottom to get rid of any browned beef bits. Add in onion, salt, bay leaf, cloves, and garlic powder. Seal the lid, press Meat/Stew, and cook on High for 15 minutes. Release the pressure quickly. Add in pumpkin and carrots without stirring.
2. Seal the lid.Cook on High Pressure for 5 minutes. Release the pressure quickly. In a bowl, mix water and cornstarch until cornstarch dissolves completely and mix into the stew. Allow to simmer on Sauté for 5 minutes until you attain the desired thickness.

Italian Beef Sandwiches

Servings: 8

Cooking Time: 65 Minutes

Ingredients:

- ¼ cup olive oil
- 1 tablespoon Italian seasoning
- 2 teaspoons hot sauce
- 1 teaspoon garlic salt
- ½ teaspoon ground black pepper
- 3 medium bell peppers, variety of colors, seeded and sliced
- 1 large yellow onion, peeled and sliced
- 1 boneless chuck roast, quartered
- 4 cups beef broth
- 8 hoagie rolls
- 1 cup chopped jarred giardiniera, drained

Directions:

1. In a large bowl, combine oil, Italian seasoning, hot sauce, garlic salt, and black pepper. Add bell peppers, onion, and roast and toss. Refrigerate covered at least 30 minutes or up to overnight.
2. Press the Sauté button on the Instant Pot and add meat, vegetables, and marinade. Sear meat 5 minutes, making sure to brown each side. Add broth. Press the Cancel button. Lock lid.
3. Press the Manual or Pressure Cook button and adjust time to 60 minutes. When timer beeps, let pressure release naturally for 5 minutes. Quick-release any additional pressure until float valve drops. Unlock lid. Strain all but ¼ cup liquid from pot. Set strained liquid aside for dipping.
4. Transfer meat to a cutting board. Let meat rest 5 minutes, then thinly slice roast and add back to pot with vegetables and remaining pot liquid to moisten meat.
5. Using a slotted spoon, transfer meat to rolls, garnish with giardiniera, and serve with dipping liquid.

Melt-in-your-mouth Meatballs

Servings: 4

Cooking Time: 16 Minutes

Ingredients:

- 1 pound 80/20 ground beef
- ¼ cup grated Parmesan cheese
- 1 large egg, lightly beaten
- 1 tablespoon Italian seasoning
- 1 cup panko bread crumbs
- ½ teaspoon garlic salt
- ½ teaspoon ground black pepper
- 2 tablespoons olive oil
- 1 cup marinara sauce
- 2 cups water

Directions:

1. In a medium bowl, combine beef, cheese, egg, Italian seasoning, bread crumbs, garlic salt, and pepper. If stiff, add 1–2 tablespoons water. Form mixture into eight meatballs. Set aside.
2. Press the Sauté button on the Instant Pot and heat oil. Place meatballs around the edge of pot. Sear all sides of meatballs, about 4 minutes total. Press the Cancel button.
3. Transfer seared meatballs to a 7-cup glass baking dish. Top with marinara sauce. Discard extra juice and oil from pot.
4. Add water to the Instant Pot and insert steam rack. Place glass baking dish on top of steam rack. Lock lid.
5. Press the Manual or Pressure Cook button and adjust time to 12 minutes. When timer beeps, let pressure release naturally for 10 minutes. Quick-release any additional pressure until float valve drops. Unlock lid.
6. Transfer meatballs to plates. Serve warm.

Fish & Seafood

Fish & Seafood

Haddock With Edamame Soybeans

Servings: 4

Cooking Time: 25 Minutes

Ingredients:

- 1 pack edamame soybeans
- 1 lb haddock fillets
- 1 clove garlic, minced
- 2 tsp grated ginger
- ¼ red chili, sliced
- 1 tbsp honey
- 2 tbsp soy sauce
- Salt and pepper to taste

Directions:

1. Pour 1 cup of water into your Instant Pot and fit in a trivet. Mix garlic, ginger, red chili, honey, soy sauce, salt, and pepper in a bowl. Add in the haddock fillets and toss to coat. Spread the fillets on a greased baking pan; scatter edamame soybeans around. Place the pan on the trivet.
2. Seal the lid. Cook on Steam for 6 minutes on High pressure. When done, allow a natural release for 10 minutes, then perform a quick pressure release. Serve.

Creole Shrimp With Okra

Servings: 2

Cooking Time: 10 Minutes

Ingredients:

- 1 lb shrimp, deveined
- 6 oz okra, trimmed
- 2 tbsp olive oil
- 1 tsp garlic powder
- ½ tsp cayenne pepper
- ½ tbsp Creole seasoning
- Salt and pepper to taste

Directions:

1. Pour 1 cup water into your Instant Pot and fit in a trivet. In a baking dish, combine shrimp, okra, olive oil, garlic powder, cayenne pepper, Creole seasoning, salt, and pepper and mix to combine. Place the dish on the trivet. Seal the lid and cook for 2 minutes on Steam on High. When ready, perform a quick pressure release. Serve.

Cilantro Cod On Millet With Peppers

Servings: 4

Cooking Time: 15 Minutes

Ingredients:

- 2 tbsp olive oil
- 1 cup millet
- 1 yellow bell pepper, diced
- 1 red bell pepper, diced
- 2 cups chicken broth
- 1 cup breadcrumbs
- 4 tbsp melted butter
- ¼ cup minced fresh cilantro
- 4 cod fillets
- 1 lemon, zested and juiced

Directions:

1. Combine oil, millet, yellow and red bell peppers in the pot, and cook for 1 minute on Sauté. Mix in the chicken broth. Place a trivet on to. In a bowl, mix crumbs, butter, cilantro, lemon zest, and juice. Spoon the bread crumb mixture evenly on the cod fillet. Lay the fish on the trivet. Seal the lid and cook on High for 6 minutes. Do a quick release and serve immediately.

Red Wine Squid

Servings: 4

Cooking Time: 25 Minutes

Ingredients:

- 2 lb squid, chopped
- 2 tbsp olive oil
- Salt and pepper to taste
- ½ cup red wine
- ½ fennel bulb, sliced
- 28 oz can crushed tomatoes
- 1 red onion, sliced
- 2 garlic cloves, minced
- 1 tsp Italian seasoning
- ½ cup parsley, chopped

Directions:

1. Mix the olive oil, squid, salt, and pepper in a bowl. Pour the red wine, tomatoes, onion, garlic, Italian seasoning, and fennel in your Instant Pot and fit in a steamer basket. Put in the squid and seal the lid. Select Manual and cook for 4 minutes on High pressure. When ready, allow a natural release for 10 minutes, then perform a quick pressure release. Serve scattered with parsley.

Trout In Herb Sauce

Servings:4

Cooking Time: 5 Minutes

Ingredients:

- Trout
- 4 (½-pound) fresh river trout
- 1 teaspoon sea salt
- 4 cups torn lettuce leaves, divided
- 1 teaspoon white wine vinegar
- ½ cup water
- Herb Sauce
- ½ cup minced fresh flat-leaf parsley
- 2 teaspoons Italian seasoning
- 1 small shallot, peeled and minced
- 2 tablespoons mayonnaise
- ½ teaspoon fresh lemon juice
- ¼ teaspoon sugar

- Pinch of salt
- 2 tablespoons sliced almonds, toasted

Directions:

1. For Trout: Rinse the trout inside and out; pat dry. Sprinkle with salt inside and out. Put 3 cups lettuce leaves in the bottom of the Instant Pot. Arrange the trout over the top of the lettuce and top fish with the remaining lettuce.
2. Pour vinegar and water into pot. Lock lid.
3. Press the Manual button and adjust time to 3 minutes. When the timer beeps, let pressure release naturally for 3 minutes. Quick-release any additional pressure until float valve drops and then unlock lid.
4. Transfer fish to a serving plate. Peel and discard the skin from the fish. Remove and discard the heads if desired.
5. For Herb Sauce: In a small bowl, mix together the parsley, Italian seasoning, shallot, mayonnaise, lemon juice, sugar, and salt. Evenly divide among the fish, spreading it over them. Sprinkle toasted almonds over the top of the sauce. Serve.

Buttery Cod With Scallions

Servings: 4

Cooking Time: 15 Minutes

Ingredients:

- 4 cod fillets
- 1 fennel bulb, sliced
- Salt and pepper to taste
- 2 tbsp scallions, chopped
- 1 lemon, cut into wedges
- 1 tbsp garlic powder
- 2 tbsp butter, melted

Directions:

1. Pour 1 cup of water into your Instant Pot; fit in a trivet. Brush the cod fillets with butter and season with garlic, salt, and pepper. Place them on the trivet and top with fennel slices. Seal the lid, Select Manual, and cook for 5 minutes on High. Once ready, perform a quick pressure release. Sprinkle with scallions and serve with lemon wedges.

Steamed Salmon Over Creamy Polenta

Servings: 4

Cooking Time: 30 Minutes

Ingredients:

- 4 salmon fillets, skin removed
- 1 cup corn grits polenta
- ½ cup coconut milk
- 3 cups chicken stock
- 3 tbsp butter
- Salt to taste
- 3 tbsp Cajun seasoning
- 1 tbsp sugar

Directions:

1. Combine polenta, milk, chicken stock, butter, and salt in the pot. In a bowl, mix Cajun seasoning, sugar, and salt. Oil the fillets with cooking spray and brush with the spice mixture. Insert a trivet in the pot and arrange the fillets on top. Seal the lid and cook on High Pressure for 9 minutes. Do a natural pressure release for 10 minutes.

Easy Seafood Paella

Servings: 4

Cooking Time: 20 Minutes

Ingredients:

- 1 cup tiger prawns, peeled and deveined
- 1 lb mussels, cleaned and debearded
- ½ tsp guindilla (cayenne pepper)
- ½ lb clams
- 2 tbsp olive oil
- 1 onion, chopped
- 2 garlic cloves, minced
- 1 red bell pepper, chopped
- 1 cup rice
- 2 cups clam juice
- ¾ cup green peas, frozen
- 1 tbsp parsley, chopped
- 1 tbsp turmeric
- 1 whole lemon, quartered

Directions:

1. Warm the olive oil in your Instant Pot on Sauté. Add in prawns, red pepper, onion, and garlic and cook for 3 minutes. Stir in rice for 1 minute and pour in clam juice, turmeric, mussels, and clams. Seal the lid, select Manual, and cook for 5 minutes on High pressure. When ready, perform a quick pressure release and unlock the lid. Stir in green peas and guindilla for 3-4 minutes. Top with lemon quarters and parsley. Serve immediately.

Indian Prawn Curry

Servings: 4

Cooking Time: 30 Minutes

Ingredients:

- 1 ½ lb prawns, deveined
- 2 tbsp ghee
- 2 garlic cloves, minced
- 1 onion, chopped
- 1 tsp ginger, grated
- ½ tsp ground turmeric
- 1 tsp red chili powder
- 2 tsp ground cumin
- 2 tsp ground coriander
- 2 tbsp curry paste
- 2 cups coconut milk
- 1 cup tomatoes, chopped
- 2 habanero peppers, minced
- Salt and pepper to taste
- 1 tbsp fresh lemon juice

Directions:

1. Melt the ghee in your Instant Pot on Sauté. Add in garlic, onion, and ginger and cook for 4 minutes. Stir in the turmeric, chili powder, cumin, coriander, and curry paste and cook for 1 more minute. Stir in coconut milk, prawns, tomatoes, habanero peppers, salt, and pepper.
2. Seal the lid. Select Manual and cook for 5 minutes on Low. Once ready, allow a natural release for 10 minutes, then perform a quick pressure release, and unlock the lid. Top with lemon juice and serve.

Low-country Boil

Servings: 6

Cooking Time: 5 Minutes

Ingredients:

- 1 large sweet onion, peeled and chopped
- 4 cloves garlic, quartered
- 6 small red potatoes, cut in sixths
- 3 ears corn, cut in thirds
- 1½ pounds fully cooked andouille sausage, cut in 1" sections
- 1 pound frozen tail-on shrimp
- 1 tablespoon Old Bay Seasoning
- 2 cups chicken broth
- 1 lemon, cut into 6 wedges
- ½ cup chopped fresh parsley

Directions:

1. Layer onions in an even layer in the Instant Pot. Scatter the garlic on top of onions. Add red potatoes in an even layer, then do the same for the corn and sausage. Add the shrimp and sprinkle with Old Bay Seasoning. Pour in broth.
2. Squeeze lemon wedges into the Instant Pot and place squeezed lemon wedges into the Instant Pot. Lock lid.
3. Press the Manual button and adjust time to 5 minutes. When timer beeps, quick-release the pressure until float valve drops and then unlock lid. Transfer ingredients to a serving platter and garnish with parsley.

Orange Roughy With Zucchini

Servings: 2

Cooking Time: 3 Minutes

Ingredients:

- 1 cup water
- 1 large zucchini, thinly sliced
- 2 orange roughy fillets, cubed
- Juice of 1 medium lemon
- 1 teaspoon salt
- ½ teaspoon ground black pepper
- 4 tablespoons unsalted butter, cut into 8 pats

- 2 tablespoons chopped fresh parsley

Directions:

1. Add water to the Instant Pot and insert steamer basket.
2. Add zucchini to basket in an even layer. Add orange roughy fillets on top. Squeeze lemon juice over fish. Season with salt and pepper. Distribute butter pats on fish and zucchini. Lock lid.
3. Press the Manual or Pressure Cook button and adjust time to 3 minutes. When timer beeps, quick-release pressure until float valve drops. Unlock lid.
4. Transfer fish and zucchini to two plates. Garnish with parsley. Serve warm.

Crab Risotto

Servings: 4

Cooking Time: 15 Minutes

Ingredients:

- 4 tablespoons unsalted butter
- 1 small yellow onion, peeled and finely diced
- 1 ½ cups Arborio rice
- 4 cups vegetable broth
- 3 tablespoons grated Parmesan cheese, divided
- ½ teaspoon garlic salt
- ¼ teaspoon ground black pepper
- 1 cup lump crabmeat, picked over for shells

Directions:

1. Press the Sauté button on the Instant Pot. Add butter and heat until melted. Add onion and stir-fry 3–5 minutes until translucent.
2. Add rice, broth, 2 tablespoons cheese, garlic salt, and pepper. Press the Cancel button. Lock lid.
3. Press the Manual or Pressure Cook button and adjust time to 10 minutes. When timer beeps, let pressure release naturally for 10 minutes. Quick-release any additional pressure until float valve drops. Unlock lid.
4. Stir in crab and remaining cheese. Serve warm.

Shrimp With Chickpeas & Olives

Servings: 6

Cooking Time: 25 Minutes

Ingredients:

- 2 lb shrimp, deveined
- 2 garlic cloves, minced
- 1 carrot, chopped
- 1 cup chickpeas, soaked
- 3 cups fish broth
- ½ cup olives, pitted
- Salt and pepper to taste
- 1 cup tomatoes, chopped
- 2 tbsp olive oil
- 1 onion, chopped

Directions:

1. Warm the olive oil in your Instant Pot on Sauté. Add in onion, garlic, carrot, salt, and pepper and cook for 4 minutes until soft. Add tomatoes, chickpeas, olives and broth. Simmer for 5 minutes. Add the shrimp and toss to coat in the sauce. Seal the lid and cook on High Pressure for 4 minutes. Release the pressure naturally. Serve warm.

Herbed Poached Salmon

Servings: 2

Cooking Time: 20 Minutes

Ingredients:

- 2 salmon fillets, skin-on
- 1 cup chicken broth
- ¼ cup dry white wine
- 1 tsp lemon zest
- ¼ tsp basil
- ¼ tsp oregano
- ¼ tsp thyme
- ¼ tsp marjoram
- 1 tbsp garlic oil
- 4 scallions, chopped
- Salt and pepper to taste

Directions:

1. Pour chicken broth and white wine in your Instant

Pot and fit in a trivet. In a bowl, combine basil, oregano, thyme, marjoram, lemon zest, garlic oil, salt, and pepper. Spread the rub evenly onto the salmon and place it on the trivet. Seal the lid, select Manual, and cook for 5 minutes on High pressure. Once over, allow a natural release for 5 minutes, perform a quick pressure release, and unlock the lid. Sprinkle with scallions and serve.

Spicy Haddock With Beer & Potatoes

Servings: 4

Cooking Time: 25 Minutes

Ingredients:

- 4 potatoes, cut into matchsticks
- 8 oz beer
- 2 eggs
- 1 cup flour
- ½ tbsp cayenne powder
- 1 tbsp cumin powder
- Salt and pepper to taste
- 4 haddock fillets
- 2 tbsp olive oil

Directions:

1. In a bowl, whisk beer and eggs. In another bowl, combine flour, cayenne, cumin, pepper, and salt. Coat each fish piece in the egg mixture, then dredge in the flour mixture, coating all sides. Grease a baking dish with cooking spray.
2. Place in the fish fillets, pour ¼ cup of water, and grease with cooking spray. Place the potatoes in the pot and cover with water and place a trivet over the potatoes. Lay the baking dish on top and seal the lid. Cook on High Pressure for 15 minutes. Do a quick release. Drain and crush the potatoes with olive oil and serve with the fish.

Spicy Pasta With Seafood

Servings: 4

Cooking Time: 20 Minutes

Ingredients:

- 2 tbsp olive oil
- 1 onion, diced
- 16 oz penne
- 24 oz arrabbiata sauce
- 3 cups chicken broth
- Salt and pepper to taste
- 16 oz scallops
- ¼ cup Parmesan, grated
- Basil leaves for garnish

Directions:

1. Heat oil on Sauté. Stir-fry onion for 3 minutes. Stir in penne, arrabbiata sauce, salt, pepper, and 2 cups of broth. Seal the lid and cook for 6 minutes on High Pressure. Do a quick release. Remove to a plate. Pour the remaining broth and add scallops. Press Sauté and cook for 4 minutes. Mix in the pasta and serve topped with Parmesan cheese and basil leaves.

Ginger & Garlic Crab

Servings: 4

Cooking Time: 15 Minutes

Ingredients:

- 1 lb crabs, halved
- 2 tbsp butter
- 1 shallot, chopped
- 1 garlic cloves, minced
- 1 cup coconut milk
- 1-inch ginger, sliced
- 1 lemongrass stalk
- Salt and pepper to taste
- 1 lemon, sliced

Directions:

1. Melt the butter in your Instant Pot on Sauté. Place in shallot, garlic, and ginger and cook for 3 minutes. Pour in coconut milk, crabs, lemongrass, salt, and pepper and seal the lid. Select Manual and cook for 6 minutes on High pressure. Once ready, perform a quick pressure release and unlock the lid. Serve with lemon slices.

Quick Shrimp Gumbo With Sausage

Servings: 4

Cooking Time: 30 Minutes

Ingredients:

- 1 lb jumbo shrimp
- 2 tbsp olive oil
- 1/3 cup flour
- 1 ½ tsp Cajun seasoning
- 1 onion, chopped
- 1 red bell pepper, chopped
- 2 celery stalks, chopped
- 2 garlic cloves, minced
- 1 serrano pepper, minced
- 2 ½ cups chicken broth
- 6 oz andouille sausage, sliced
- 2 green onions, finely sliced
- Salt and pepper to taste

Directions:

1. Heat olive oil on Sauté. Whisk in the flour with a wooden spoon and cook 3 minutes, stirring constantly. Stir in Cajun seasoning, onion, bell pepper, celery, garlic, and serrano pepper for about 5 minutes. Pour in the chicken broth, ¾ cup water, and andouille sausage. Seal and cook for 6 minutes on High Pressure. Do a natural pressure for 5 minutes. Stir the shrimp into the gumbo to eat it up for 3 minutes. Adjust the seasoning. Ladle the gumbo into bowls and garnish with the green onions.

Creamed Crab Sauce

Servings: 4

Cooking Time: 5 Minutes

Ingredients:

- 2 tablespoons unsalted butter
- ¼ cup finely diced red onion
- 1 pound lump crabmeat
- ¼ cup chicken broth
- 6 ounces cream cheese, softened
- 2 teaspoons cooking sherry
- 1 tablespoon all-purpose flour
- ½ teaspoon salt
- ½ teaspoon ground black pepper

Directions:

1. Press the Sauté button on the Instant Pot. Add butter and heat until melted. Add onion; stir-fry 3–5 minutes until onions begin to soften.
2. Stir crabmeat and broth into pot. Press the Cancel button. Lock lid.
3. Press the Steam button on the Instant Pot and adjust time to 0 minutes. When timer beeps, quick-release pressure until float valve drops. Unlock lid.
4. Stir in cream cheese, sherry, flour, salt, and pepper. Transfer to a serving bowl. Let sit 10 minutes to thicken. Serve warm.

Tilapia With Basil Pesto & Rice

Servings: 2

Cooking Time: 15 Minutes

Ingredients:

- 2 tilapia fillets
- 2 tbsp basil pesto
- ½ cup basmati rice
- Salt and pepper to taste

Directions:

1. Place the rice and 1 cup of water in your Instant Pot and season with salt and pepper; fit in a trivet. Place tilapia fillets in the middle of a parchment paper sheet. Top each fillet with pesto and roll all the edges to form a packet. Place it on the trivet and seal the lid.
2. Select Manual and cook for 6 minutes on Low pressure. Once ready, perform a quick pressure release. Carefully unlock the lid. Fluff the rice with a fork and transfer to a plate. Top with tilapia and serve.

Basil Salmon With Artichokes & Potatoes

Servings: 4

Cooking Time: 25 Minutes

Ingredients:

- 1 cup artichoke hearts, halved
- 4 salmon fillets
- 1 lb new potatoes
- 2 tbsp butter
- Salt and pepper to taste
- 2 tbsp basil, chopped

Directions:

1. Season the potatoes with salt and pepper. Pour 1 cup of water into your Instant Pot and fit in a trivet. Place the potatoes on the trivet and seal the lid. Select Manual and cook for 2 minutes on High pressure. Once over, perform a quick pressure release and unlock the lid. Sprinkle the salmon and artichokes with salt and pepper. Put them on the trivet with the potatoes, sprinkle with basil, and seal the lid. Select Manual and cook for another 5 minutes on High pressure. Once done, allow a natural release for 10 minutes. Remove potatoes to a bowl and stir in butter. Serve the salmon with artichokes and potatoes.

Mackerel With Potatoes & Spinach

Servings: 4

Cooking Time: 20 Minutes

Ingredients:

- 4 mackerels, skin on
- 1 lb spinach, torn
- 5 potatoes, peeled, chopped
- 3 tbsp olive oil
- 2 garlic cloves, crushed
- 2 tbsp mint leaves, chopped
- 1 lemon, juiced
- Sea salt to taste

Directions:

1. Heat 2 tbsp of the olive oil on Sauté. Stir-fry garlic for 1 minute. Stir in spinach and salt and cook for 4-5 minutes until wilted; set aside. Make a layer of potatoes in the pot. Top with fish and drizzle with lemon juice, remaining olive oil, and salt. Pour in 1 cup of water, seal the lid, and cook on Steam for 7 minutes on High. When ready, do a quick release. Carefully unlock the lid. Plate the fish and potatoes with spinach and serve topped with mint leaves.

Herby Crab Legs With Lemon

Servings: 4

Cooking Time: 10 Minutes

Ingredients:

- 3 lb king crab legs, broken in half
- 1 tsp rosemary
- 1 tsp thyme
- 1 tsp dill
- ¼ cup butter, melted
- Salt and pepper to taste
- 1 lemon, cut into wedges

Directions:

1. Pour 1 cup of water into your Instant Pot and fit in a trivet. Season the crab legs with rosemary, thyme, dill, salt, and pepper; place on the trivet. Seal the lid, select Manual, and cook for 3 minutes. When ready, perform a quick pressure release. Remove crab legs to a bowl and drizzle with melted butter. Serve with lemon wedges.

Dijon Catfish Fillets With White Wine

Servings: 3

Cooking Time: 15 Minutes + Cooling Time

Ingredients:

- 1 lb catfish fillets
- 1 lemon, juiced
- ½ cup parsley, chopped
- 2 garlic cloves, crushed
- 1 onion, finely chopped
- 1 tbsp dill, chopped
- 1 tbsp rosemary, chopped
- 2 cups white wine
- 2 tbsp Dijon mustard
- 1 cup extra virgin olive oil

Directions:

1. In a bowl, mix lemon juice, parsley, garlic, onion, dill, rosemary, wine, mustard, and oil. Stir well. Submerge the fillets and cover with a tight lid. Refrigerate for 1 hour. Insert a trivet in the Instant Pot. Remove the fish from the fridge and place it on the rack. Pour in 1 cup of water and marinade. Seal the lid. Cook on Steam for 8 minutes on High. Release the pressure quickly. Serve immediately.

Herby Trout With Farro & Green Beans

Servings: 4

Cooking Time: 20 Minutes

Ingredients:

- 1 cup farro
- 2 cups water
- 4 skinless trout fillets
- 8 oz green beans
- 1 tbsp olive oil
- Salt and pepper to taste
- 4 tbsp melted butter
- ½ tbsp sugar
- ½ tbsp lemon juice
- ½ tsp dried rosemary
- 2 garlic cloves, minced
- ½ tsp dried thyme

Directions:

1. Pour the farro and water into the pot and mix with green beans and olive oil. Season with salt and black pepper. In another bowl, mix the remaining black pepper and salt, butter, sugar, lemon juice, rosemary, garlic, and thyme.
2. Coat the trout with the buttery herb sauce. Insert a trivet in the pot and lay the trout fillets on the trivet. Seal the lid and cook on High Pressure for 12 minutes. Do a quick release and serve immediately.

Salmon & Broccoli Salad

Servings: 2

Cooking Time: 15 Minutes

Ingredients:

- 2 salmon fillet
- 8 oz broccoli
- 2 mini bell peppers, chopped
- Salt and pepper to taste
- ½ lemon, juiced
- 2 tbsp olive oil
- 1 gem lettuce, torn

Directions:

1. Pour 1 cup of water into your Instant Pot and fit in a trivet. Chop broccoli into florets and transfer to a greased baking dish with the peppers. Add in the salmon and place the dish on the trivet; sprinkle with salt and pepper.
2. Seal the lid and cook for 5 minutes on Steam. When ready, perform a quick pressure release. Place the lettuce in a serving bowl, add in broccoli, peppers, olive oil, lemon juice, and salt. Top with the salmon and serve.

Salmon With Green Beans & Rice

Servings: 4

Cooking Time: 20 Minutes

Ingredients:

- 1 cup rice
- 2 cups vegetable stock
- 4 skinless salmon fillets
- 1 cup green beans, chopped
- 3 tbsp olive oil
- Salt and pepper to taste
- 2 limes, juiced
- 1 tsp sweet paprika
- 2 jalapeño peppers, diced
- 2 garlic cloves, minced
- ½ cup corn kernels
- 2 tbsp chopped fresh dill

Directions:

1. Add rice, stock, and salt to your Instant Pot. Place a trivet over the rice. In a bowl, mix oil, lime juice, paprika, jalapeño, garlic, and dill. Coat the fish with the dill sauce while reserving a little for garnishing. Lay the salmon fillets on the trivet. Seal the lid and cook on High Pressure for 8 minutes. Do a quick release. Fluff the rice with a fork and mix in the green beans and corn kernels. Transfer to a serving plate and top with the salmon. Drizzle with the remaining dill sauce and serve.

White Wine Marinated Squid Rings

Servings: 3

Cooking Time: 25 Minutes + Cooling Time

Ingredients:

- 1 lb fresh squid rings
- 1 cup dry white wine
- 1 cup olive oil
- 2 garlic cloves, crushed
- 1 lemon, juiced
- 2 cups fish stock
- ¼ tsp red pepper flakes
- ¼ tsp dried oregano
- 1 tbsp rosemary, chopped
- 1 tsp sea salt

Directions:

1. In a bowl, mix wine, olive oil, lemon juice, garlic, flakes, oregano, rosemary, and salt. Submerge squid rings in this mixture and cover with a lid. Refrigerate for 1 hour. Remove the squid from the fridge and place it in the pot along with stock and half of the marinade. Seal the lid. Cook on High Pressure for 6 minutes. Release the pressure naturally for 10 minutes. Transfer the rings to a plate and drizzle with some marinade to serve.

Salmon With Coconut Rice

Servings: 2

Cooking Time: 20 Minutes

Ingredients:

- 1 oz vegetable soup mix, dried
- 2 salmon fillets
- ½ cup jasmine rice
- 1 cup coconut milk
- 1 tbsp ghee
- ½ oz grated ginger
- 1 spring onion, chopped
- Salt and pepper to taste

Directions:

1. Stir the rice, coconut milk, ghee, ginger, and soup mix in your Instant Pot and fit in a trivet. Season salmon with salt and pepper and place it on the trivet. Seal the lid, select Manual, and cook for 5 minutes on High pressure. Once done, allow a natural release for 10 minutes and unlock the lid. Serve topped with spring onion.

Lemon Salmon With Blue Cheese

Servings: 4

Cooking Time: 15 Minutes

Ingredients:

- 1 lb salmon fillets
- 2 tbsp olive oil
- 1 garlic clove, minced
- 1 tbsp lemon juice
- ¼ tsp thyme
- 1 tbsp blue cheese, crumbled
- 1 lemon, sliced
- 2 sprigs fresh rosemary
- Salt and pepper to taste

Directions:

1. Mix the olive oil, garlic, lemon juice, thyme, salt, pepper, and blue cheese in a bowl. Pour 1 cup of water into your Instant Pot and fit in a trivet. Place salmon on the trivet and top with cheese mixture, lemon slices, and rosemary sprigs. Seal the lid, select Manual, and cook for 5 minutes on High pressure. When done, perform a quick pressure release and unlock the lid. Discard the rosemary sprigs and serve.

Poultry

Poultry

Chicken Salad

Servings: 6

Cooking Time: 15 Minutes

Ingredients:

- 1 cup chicken broth
- 2 pounds boneless, skinless chicken breasts
- 2 medium stalks celery, diced
- 1 cup chopped pecans
- 1 ½ cups mayonnaise
- 1 tablespoon Dijon mustard
- ½ teaspoon salt
- ¼ teaspoon ground black pepper

Directions:

1. Add broth and chicken to the Instant Pot. Lock lid.
2. Press the Manual or Pressure Cook button and adjust time to 15 minutes. When timer beeps, let pressure release naturally for 10 minutes. Quick-release any additional pressure until float valve drops. Unlock lid. Check chicken using a meat thermometer to ensure the internal temperature is at least 165°F.
3. Using two forks, pull apart chicken in pot.
4. Using a slotted spoon, transfer chicken to a large bowl. Stir in remaining ingredients. Refrigerate until chilled. Serve.

Fabulous Orange Chicken Stew

Servings: 4

Cooking Time: 55 Minutes

Ingredients:

- 1 cup fire-roasted tomatoes, diced
- 1 lb chicken breasts
- 1 tbsp chili powder
- Salt and pepper to taste
- 1 cup orange juice
- 2 cups chicken broth

Directions:

1. Season the chicken with chili powder, salt, and pepper, and place in your Instant Pot. Add fire-roasted tomatoes and cook on Sauté for 10 minutes, stirring occasionally. Pour in the broth and orange juice. Seal the lid and cook on Poultry for 25 minutes on High. Release the pressure naturally for 10 minutes. Serve immediately.

Potato & Cauliflower Turkey Soup

Servings: 4

Cooking Time: 35 Minutes

Ingredients:

- 1 tbsp olive oil
- 1 lb ground turkey
- 2 garlic cloves, minced
- 1 leek, chopped
- 1 cup cauliflower florets
- 1 carrot, chopped
- 1 celery stalk, chopped
- 1 cup tomato sauce
- ½ tsp dried sage
- ½ tsp dried thyme
- 4 cups chicken broth
- 3 potatoes, chopped
- Salt and pepper to taste

Directions:

1. Warm the olive oil in your Instant Pot on Sauté. Place the ground turkey and garlic and cook for 5-6 minutes. Remove to a bowl. Add the leek, carrot, celery, cauliflower, tomato sauce, chicken broth, potatoes, sage, and thyme to the pot and return the turkey. Seal the lid, select Manual, and cook for 8 minutes on High. When over, allow a natural release for 10 minutes and unlock the lid. Sprinkle with salt and pepper. Serve right away.

Chicken Fricassee

Servings: 4

Cooking Time: 40 Minutes

Ingredients:

- 4 chicken breasts
- 2 tbsp olive oil
- 1 onion, chopped
- 2 garlic cloves, minced
- Salt and pepper to taste
- ½ cup dry white wine
- ½ cup chicken broth
- ¼ cup heavy cream
- 2 tbsp capers
- 1 bay leaf
- 2 tbsp tarragon, chopped

Directions:

1. Warm the olive oil in your Instant Pot on Sauté. Sprinkle chicken with salt and pepper and place in the pot. Cook for 6 minutes on all sides. Add in onion and garlic and cook for 3 minutes. Pour in chicken broth, white wine, and bay leaf. Seal the lid, select Manual, and cook for 15 minutes on High pressure.
2. When ready, perform a quick pressure release. Remove bay leaf and put in heavy cream and capers. Stir for 2-3 minutes and cook in the residual heat until thoroughly warmed. Ladle into bowls, top with tarragon, and serve.

Spicy Turkey Casserole With Tomatoes

Servings: 4

Cooking Time: 30 Minutes

Ingredients:

- 2 cans fire-roasted tomatoes
- 2 bell peppers, cut into thick strips
- 2 tbsp olive oil
- ½ sweet onion, diced
- 3 cloves garlic, minced
- 1 jalapeño pepper, minced
- 1 lb turkey breast, cubed
- 1 cup salsa
- 2 tsp chili powder
- 1 tsp ground cumin
- Salt to taste
- 1 tbsp oregano, chopped

Directions:

1. Warm oil on Sauté. Add in garlic, onion, and jalapeño and cook for 5 minutes until fragrant. Stir in turkey and cook for 5-6 minutes until browned. Add in salsa, tomatoes, bell peppers, and 1 ½ cups water. Season with salt, cumin, and chili powder. Seal the lid, press Manual, and cook for 10 minutes on High. Release the pressure quickly. Top with oregano and serve.

Sage Turkey & Red Wine Casserole

Servings: 4

Cooking Time: 50 Minutes

Ingredients:

- 1 lb boneless turkey breast, cubed
- 1 onion, sliced
- 1 celery stalk, sliced
- 2 tbsp olive oil
- 1 carrot, diced
- ½ cup red wine
- Salt and pepper to taste
- 1 cup chicken broth
- 1 tbsp tomato puree
- 2 tbsp sage, chopped

Directions:

1. Warm olive oil in your IP on Sauté. Add in the turkey cubes and brown for 4-5 minutes, stirring occasionally; set aside. Add onion, celery, and carrot to the pot and sauté for 3-4 minutes. Stir in tomato puree, red wine, salt, and pepper and pour in chicken broth. Stir and return the turkey. Seal the lid, select Manual, and cook for 20 minutes on High. Once ready, release pressure naturally for 10 minutes. Unlock the lid, top with sage and serve.

Turkey With Rice & Peas

Servings: 6

Cooking Time: 45 Minutes

Ingredients:

- 1 ½ lb turkey breasts, sliced
- 1 tbsp olive oil
- 1 small onion, sliced
- 1 cup brown rice
- 1 cup green peas
- 2 cups chicken broth
- Salt and pepper to taste

Directions:

1. Warm the olive oil in your Instant Pot on Sauté. Add in the onion and turkey and cook for 3 minutes, stirring occasionally. Stir in rice for 1 minute and pour in the broth; season with salt and pepper. Seal the lid, select Manual, and cook for 20 minutes on High.
2. Once ready, allow a natural release for 10 minutes, then perform a quick pressure release and unlock the lid. Mix in green peas and cook for 3-4 minutes on Sauté. Serve.

Lemon-butter Chicken And Fingerling Potatoes

Servings:8

Cooking Time: 10 Minutes

Ingredients:

- 3 pounds boneless and skinless chicken thighs
- 1 teaspoon salt
- ½ teaspoon ground black pepper
- 2 pounds fingerling potatoes, halved
- 1 large sweet onion, peeled and large-chopped
- 1 cup chicken broth
- 1 medium lemon, halved, divided
- 4 tablespoons unsalted butter, cut into 8 pats, divided

Directions:

1. Season chicken with salt and pepper.

2. Layer potatoes and onion in the Instant Pot. Pour in broth. Place chicken on top. Squeeze half of lemon over chicken. Add 4 butter pats. Lock lid.
3. Press the Manual or Pressure Cook button and adjust time to 10 minutes. When timer beeps, let pressure release naturally for 10 minutes. Quick-release any additional pressure until float valve drops. Unlock lid. Check chicken using a meat thermometer to make sure internal temperature is at least 165°F.
4. Using a slotted spoon, remove chicken, potatoes, and onions and transfer to a platter. Squeeze remaining half of lemon over platter. Top with remaining 4 butter pats. Serve warm.

Thyme Chicken With White Wine

Servings: 6

Cooking Time: 45 Minutes

Ingredients:

- 1 cup chicken stock
- ½ cup white wine
- ½ onion, chopped
- 2 cloves garlic, minced
- 3.5-pound whole chicken
- Salt and pepper to taste
- ½ tsp dried thyme
- 3 tbsp butter, melted
- ½ tsp paprika

Directions:

1. Into your Instant Pot, add onion, stock, wine, and garlic. Over the mixture, place a steamer rack. Rub pepper, salt, and thyme onto chicken. Put it on the rack breast-side up. Seal the lid, press Manual, and cook for 26 minutes. Release the pressure quickly. Preheat oven broiler. In a bowl, mix paprika and butter. Remove the chicken from your pot. Get rid of onion and stock. Brush butter mixture onto the chicken and cook under the broiler for 5 minutes until chicken skin is crispy and browned. Set chicken to a cutting board to cool for about 5 minutes, then carve, and transfer to a serving platter. Serve.

Beer Can Chicken Dijon

Servings: 5

Cooking Time: 20 Minutes

Ingredients:

- ¼ cup Dijon mustard
- 3 pounds chicken legs/drumsticks
- 1 large onion, peeled and chopped
- 1 bottle beer, any brand/variety

Directions:

1. Rub Dijon mustard over the chicken legs.
2. Scatter onion in Instant Pot. Insert trivet. Add beer. Press the Sauté button and simmer unlidded for 5 minutes (press the Adjust button to change the temperature to Less if mixture starts to boil too vigorously). Arrange chicken standing up, meaty-side down, on the trivet. Lock lid.
3. Press the Poultry button and cook for the default time of 15 minutes. When timer beeps, let pressure release naturally for 10 minutes. Quick-release any additional pressure until float valve drops and then unlock lid. Check the chicken using a meat thermometer to ensure the internal temperature is at least 165°F.
4. Remove chicken from pot and serve.

Chili Lime Chicken

Servings: 8

Cooking Time: 10 Minutes

Ingredients:

- ½ cup fresh lime juice
- Zest from 1 lime
- ¼ cup olive oil
- 2 small jalapeños, seeded and finely chopped
- 3 garlic cloves, minced
- 2 tablespoons honey
- 2 teaspoons sea salt
- 2 teaspoons chili powder
- ¼ cup finely chopped fresh cilantro
- 3 pounds boneless chicken thighs
- 1 cup chicken broth

Directions:

1. In a large bowl, combine all ingredients except for chicken and chicken broth.
2. Pat chicken thighs dry with a paper towel. Toss chicken into marinade. Cover and refrigerate overnight.
3. Place trivet in Instant Pot. Place steamer basket on trivet. Pour in chicken broth. Arrange thighs on steamer basket and pour extra marinade over the thighs. Lock lid.
4. Press the Manual button and adjust time to 10 minutes. When timer beeps, let pressure release naturally for 10 minutes. Quick-release any additional pressure until float valve drops and then unlock lid. Check the chicken using a meat thermometer to ensure the internal temperature is at least 165°F.
5. Transfer chicken to plates and serve warm.

Sweet & Spicy Bbq Chicken

Servings: 4

Cooking Time: 35 Minutes

Ingredients:

- 6 chicken drumsticks
- 1 tbsp olive oil
- 1 onion, chopped
- 1 tsp garlic, minced
- 1 jalapeño pepper, minced
- ½ cup sweet BBQ sauce
- 1 tbsp arrowroot

Directions:

1. Warm the olive oil in your Instant Pot on Sauté. Add in the onion and cook for 3 minutes. Add in garlic and jalapeño pepper and cook for another minute. Stir in barbecue sauce and 1/2 cup of water. Put in chicken drumsticks and seal the lid. Select Manual and cook for 18 minutes on High pressure. When over, perform a quick pressure release and unlock the lid. Mix 2 tbsp of water and arrowroot and pour it into the pot. Cook for 5 minutes on Sauté until the liquid thickens. Top with sauce and serve.

Chicken Wings In Yogurt-garlic Sauce

Servings: 6

Cooking Time: 35 Minutes

Ingredients:

- 12 chicken wings
- 3 tbsp olive oil
- Salt to taste
- 3 cups chicken broth
- ½ cup sour cream
- 1 cup yogurt
- 2 garlic cloves, minced

Directions:

1. Heat oil on Sauté in your Instant Pot. Brown the wings for 6 minutes, turning once. Pour in broth, salt, and seal the lid. Cook on Poultry for 15 minutes on High. Do a natural release. Unlock the lid. In a bowl, mix sour cream, yogurt, salt, and garlic. Drizzle with yogurt sauce. Serve.

Pickleback Wings

Servings:6

Cooking Time: 16 Minutes

Ingredients:

- 2 pounds chicken wings
- 1 cup dill pickle juice
- 1 tablespoon packed dark brown sugar
- 1 tablespoon hot sauce
- ¼ teaspoon garlic salt
- ¼ teaspoon ground black pepper
- ½ cup bourbon whiskey
- 1 cup dill pickle slices

Directions:

1. In a medium bowl, combine chicken wings and pickle juice. Refrigerate 1 hour.
2. In a large bowl, combine brown sugar, hot sauce, garlic salt, and pepper. Set aside.
3. If you buy chicken wings that are connected, cut them at the joint to separate. Set aside.

4. Add chicken wings, pickle juice brine, and bourbon whiskey to the Instant Pot. Lock lid.
5. Press the Manual or Pressure Cook button and adjust time to 10 minutes. When timer beeps, let pressure release naturally for 5 minutes. Quick-release any additional pressure until float valve drops. Unlock lid.
6. Add chicken wings to spice mixture and toss. Line a baking sheet with parchment paper. Transfer wings to prepared baking sheet. Broil 3 minutes. Flip wings and broil for an additional 3 minutes.
7. Transfer wings to a plate and garnish with pickle slices. Serve warm.

Roast Goose With White Wine

Servings: 4

Cooking Time: 40 Minutes

Ingredients:

- 1 lb goose fillets, sliced
- 1 onion, chopped
- 4 tbsp butter, softened
- 2 garlic cloves, crushed
- 1 cup white wine
- 2 tbsp fresh celery, chopped
- 1 tsp dried thyme
- Salt and pepper to taste

Directions:

1. Season the goose with salt and white pepper. Melt butter on Sauté in your Instant Pot and stir-fry onions, celery, and garlic for 3-4 minutes. Add the goose fillets and brown on both sides for 6-8 minutes. Add in the white wine and thyme. Pour in 1 cup of water, seal the lid, and set to Meat/Stew. Cook for 25 minutes on High Pressure. When ready, do a quick release and set aside. Serve.

Country Chicken With Vegetables

Servings: 4

Cooking Time: 30 Minutes

Ingredients:

- 4 boneless, skinless chicken thighs
- 1 cup quartered cremini mushrooms
- Salt and pepper to taste
- 2 tbsp olive oil
- 2 chopped carrots
- ½ lb green peas
- 1 chopped onion
- 3 garlic cloves, smashed
- 1 tbsp tomato paste
- 10 cherry tomatoes, halved
- ½ cup pitted green olives
- ½ cup fresh basil, minced
- ¼ cup parsley, chopped

Directions:

1. Sprinkle chicken thighs with salt and pepper. Warm the olive oil in your Instant Pot on Sauté and cook carrots, mushrooms, and onion for 5 minutes. Add in garlic and tomato paste and cook for another 30 seconds. Stir in cherry tomatoes, chicken thighs, and olives.
2. Pour in 1 cup of water. Seal the lid, select Manual, and cook for 10 minutes on High pressure. Once ready, perform a quick pressure release and unlock the lid. Select Sauté and mix in green peas; cook for 5 minutes. Serve topped with fresh basil and parsley.

Spicy Chicken Thighs

Servings: 4

Cooking Time: 45 Minutes

Ingredients:

- 1 lb chicken thighs
- 2 tbsp oil
- 4 cups chicken broth
- 1 tsp salt

- 2 tsp lime zest
- 1 tsp chili powder
- ½ cup tomato puree
- 1 tbsp sugar

Directions:

1. Season the meat evenly with salt and chili powder on both sides. Warm oil on Sauté and add the thighs. Brown on both sides and then set aside. Add the tomato puree, sugar, and lime zest. Cook for 10 minutes to obtain a thick sauce. Add the chicken and pour in the broth. Seal the lid and cook on Poultry for 20 minutes on High pressure. Do a quick release. Unlock the lid. Serve.

Buffalo Chicken Wraps

Servings:8

Cooking Time: 20 Minutes

Ingredients:

- 2 cups buffalo wing sauce
- 2 tablespoons melted butter
- 2 pounds chicken breasts, halved
- 8 flour tortillas
- 1 cup finely diced celery, divided
- 8 tablespoons blue cheese dressing

Directions:

1. In a large bowl, whisk together wing sauce and butter. Add chicken breasts and toss to coat. Place chicken and all of the sauce in the Instant Pot. Lock lid.
2. Press the Manual button and adjust time to 20 minutes. When the timer beeps, let pressure release naturally for 10 minutes. Quick-release any additional pressure until float valve drops and then unlock lid. Check the chicken using a meat thermometer to ensure the internal temperature is at least 165°F.
3. With the chicken still in the Instant Pot, use two forks and pull the chicken apart; mix with juices in the Instant Pot.
4. To assemble the wraps, use a slotted spoon to place ⅛ of the chicken mixture on each tortilla. Top each tortilla with ⅛ cup celery, and 1 tablespoon dressing. Fold the wraps and serve.

Turkey Meatball Soup With Rice

Servings: 4

Cooking Time: 30 Minutes

Ingredients:

- 1 green bell pepper, chopped
- 1 habanero pepper, seeded and minced
- 2 tbsp olive oil
- 1 onion, chopped
- 2 garlic cloves, minced
- ½ lb ground turkey
- 1 carrot, chopped
- 1 can diced tomatoes
- ½ tsp cumin
- ½ tsp oregano
- ½ cup white rice, rinsed
- Salt and pepper to taste
- 1 egg, beaten
- 1 cup yogurt

Directions:

1. Mix ground turkey with cumin, oregano, salt, and pepper in a bowl. Shape the mixture into 1-inch balls. Warm olive oil in your Instant Pot on Sauté. Add in onion, bell pepper, habanero pepper, carrot, and garlic. Cook for 3-4 minutes. Add in meatballs, tomatoes, 3 cups water, and rice. Seal the lid, select Manual and cook for 15 minutes.
2. Once ready, perform a quick pressure release and unlock the lid. Mix the egg and yogurt in a bowl, and temper with one cup of the soup liquid, adding it slowly and whisking constantly to prevent the egg from cooking. Stir this mixture into the pot. Ladle the soup into bowls and serve immediately.

Chicken Paprikash

Servings:4

Cooking Time: 25 Minutes

Ingredients:

- 2 tablespoons ghee
- 1 medium onion, peeled and diced
- 1 small green bell pepper, seeded and diced
- 4 cloves garlic, minced
- 4 skin-on chicken breast halves
- 1 large tomato, diced
- ¼ cup tomato sauce
- 2 tablespoons Hungarian paprika
- 1 cup chicken broth
- 1 tablespoon flour
- ¾ cup sour cream
- ½ teaspoon sea salt
- ¼ teaspoon ground black pepper

Directions:

1. Press the Sauté button on the Instant Pot and heat ghee. Add onion and green pepper and sauté for 3–5 minutes until onions are translucent. Stir in garlic. Add the chicken breast skin-side down and brown for 3–4 minutes. Sprinkle the diced tomato over the chicken.
2. In a medium bowl, whisk together tomato sauce, paprika, and chicken broth. Pour over chicken. Lock lid.
3. Press the Poultry button and cook for the default time of 15 minutes. When timer beeps, let pressure release naturally for 10 minutes. Quick-release any additional pressure until float valve drops and then unlock lid. Check the chicken using a meat thermometer to ensure the internal temperature is at least 165°F. Transfer chicken to a serving platter.
4. Whisk flour and sour cream into the juices in the Instant Pot. Press the Sauté button, press the Adjust button to change the temperature to Less, and simmer unlidded for 5 minutes until sauce thickens. Season with salt and pepper. Pour sauce over chicken and serve warm.

Thai Chicken

Servings: 4

Cooking Time: 25 Minutes

Ingredients:

- 1 lb chicken thighs
- 1 cup lime juice
- 4 tbsp red curry paste
- ½ cup fish sauce
- 2 tbsp brown sugar
- 1 red chili pepper, sliced
- 2 tbsp olive oil
- 1 tsp ginger, grated
- 2 tbsp cilantro, chopped

Directions:

1. Combine lime juice, red curry paste, fish sauce, olive oil, brown sugar, ginger, and cilantro in a bowl. Add in chicken thighs and toss to coat. Transfer to your Instant Pot and pour in 1 cup water.
2. Seal the lid, select Manual, and cook for 15 minutes on High. When done, perform a quick pressure release. Top with red chili slices and serve.

Hungarian-style Turkey Stew

Servings: 4

Cooking Time: 40 Minutes

Ingredients:

- 1 lb chopped turkey pieces
- 2 tbsp butter
- 1 tsp paprika
- 1 can diced tomatoes
- 1 red onion, sliced
- 2 garlic cloves, chopped
- 1 red bell pepper, chopped
- 1 green bell pepper, chopped
- 1 cup chicken stock
- Salt and pepper to taste
- 6 tbsp sour cream
- 2 tbsp parsley, chopped

Directions:

1. Melt butter in your Instant Pot on Sauté and cook the turkey for 5 minutes, stirring occasionally. Add in onion, garlic, and bell peppers and sauté for another 3 minutes. Stir in paprika, tomatoes, and stock and seal the lid. Select Manual and cook for 20 minutes on High pressure. Once over, perform a quick pressure release and unlock the lid. Adjust the seasoning. Top with sour cream and parsley.

Easy Chicken With Capers & Tomatoes

Servings: 4

Cooking Time: 35 Minutes

Ingredients:

- 4 chicken legs
- Salt and pepper to taste
- 2 tbsp olive oil
- 1 onion, diced
- 2 garlic cloves, minced
- 1/3 cup red wine
- 2 cups diced tomatoes
- 1/3 cup capers
- 2 pickles, chopped

Directions:

1. Sprinkle pepper and salt over the chicken. Warm oil on Sauté in your Instant Pot. Add in onion and Sauté for 3 minutes until fragrant. Add in garlic and cook for 30 seconds. Mix the chicken with vegetables and cook for 6 to 7 minutes until lightly browned.
2. Add the red wine to the pan to deglaze, scraping the pan's bottom to eliminate any browned bits of food. Stir in tomatoes. Seal the lid and cook on High Pressure for 12 minutes. Release the pressure quickly. To the chicken mixture, add the capers and pickles. Serve the chicken topped with the tomato sauce and enjoy!

Garlic Chicken

Servings: 4

Cooking Time: 35 Minutes

Ingredients:

- 1 lb chicken breasts
- Salt and pepper to taste
- 2 tbsp butter
- 1 cup chicken broth
- 2 garlic cloves, minced
- 2 tbsp tarragon, chopped

Directions:

1. Place chicken breasts in your Instant Pot. Sprinkle with garlic, salt, and pepper. Pour in the chicken broth and butter. Seal the lid, select Manual, and cook for 15 minutes on High pressure.
2. When over, allow a natural release for 10 minutes and unlock the lid. Remove the chicken and shred it. Top with tarragon and serve.

Turkey Cakes With Ginger Gravy

Servings: 4

Cooking Time: 25 Minutes

Ingredients:

- 1 lb ground turkey
- ¼ cup breadcrumbs
- ¼ cup grated Parmesan
- ½ tsp garlic powder
- 2 green onions, chopped
- Salt and pepper to taste
- 2 tbsp olive oil
- 2 cups tomatoes, diced
- ¼ cup chicken broth
- Ginger sauce
- 4 tbsp soy sauce
- 2 tbsp canola oil
- 2 tbsp rice vinegar
- 1 garlic clove, minced
- 1 tsp ginger, grated
- ½ tbsp honey
- ¼ tsp black pepper
- ½ tbsp cornstarch

Directions:

1. Combine turkey, breadcrumbs, green onions, garlic powder, salt, pepper, and Parmesan cheese in a bowl. Mix with your hands and shape meatballs out of the mixture. In another bowl, mix soy sauce, canola oil, rice vinegar, garlic clove, ginger, honey, pepper, and cornstarch. Warm the olive oil in your Instant Pot on Sauté.
2. Place in meatballs and cook for 4 minutes on all sides. Pour in ginger gravy, tomatoes, and chicken stock and seal the lid. Select Manual and cook for 10 minutes on High pressure. Once over, perform a quick pressure release and unlock the lid. Serve in individual bowls.

Chicken Marinara And Zucchini

Servings: 4

Cooking Time: 15 Minutes

Ingredients:

- 2 large zucchini, diced large
- 4 chicken breast halves
- 3 cups marinara sauce
- 1 tablespoon Italian seasoning
- ½ teaspoon sea salt
- 1 cup shredded mozzarella

Directions:

1. Scatter zucchini into Instant Pot. Place chicken on zucchini. Pour marinara sauce over chicken. Sprinkle with Italian seasoning and salt. Lock lid.
2. Press the Poultry button and cook for the default time of 15 minutes. When timer beeps, let pressure release naturally for 10 minutes. Quick-release any additional pressure until float valve drops and then unlock lid. Check chicken using a meat thermometer to ensure the internal temperature is at least 165°F.
3. Sprinkle chicken with mozzarella. Press Keep Warm button, lock lid back in place, and warm for 5 minutes to allow the cheese to melt.
4. Transfer chicken and zucchini to a serving platter.

Tarragon & Garlic Chicken

Servings: 4

Cooking Time: 30 Minutes

Ingredients:

- 1 ¼ lb chicken breasts
- Salt and pepper to taste
- 2 garlic cloves, crushed
- 3 tbsp tarragon, chopped
- 2 tbsp olive oil
- 1 onion, finely chopped

Directions:

1. Warm oil on Sauté in your Instant Pot. Stir-fry the onion and garlic for 3 minutes until fragrant. Add in the chicken, salt, and pepper. Pour in 2 cups of water and adjust the seasoning. Seal the lid and cook on High Pressure for 15 minutes. When ready, do a quick pressure release. Slice the chicken and serve topped with fresh tarragon.

Pesto Chicken With Green Beans

Servings: 4

Cooking Time: 30 Minutes

Ingredients:

- 4 chicken breasts
- 2 tbsp olive oil
- ¼ cup dry white wine
- ¾ cup chicken stock
- Salt and pepper to taste
- 1 cup green beans, chopped
- For pesto
- 1 cup fresh basil
- 1 garlic clove, smashed
- 2 tbsp pine nuts
- ¼ cup Parmesan cheese
- ¼ cup extra virgin olive oil
- Salt and pepper to taste

Directions:

1. First, make the pesto - in a bowl, mix fresh basil, pine nuts, garlic, salt, pepper, and Parmesan cheese and place in a food processor. Add in oil

and process until the desired consistency is attained. Apply a thin layer of pesto to one side of each chicken breast; tightly roll into a cylinder and fasten closed with small skewers.

2. Press Sauté. Heat oil in your Instant Pot. Cook chicken rolls for 1 to 2 minutes per side until browned. Add in wine and cook until the wine has evaporated, about 3-4 minutes. Add stock, salt and pepper, and top the chicken with green beans. Seal the lid, press Meat/Stew, and cook at High Pressure for 5 minutes. Release the pressure quickly. Serve chicken rolls with cooking liquid and green beans.

Rigatoni With Turkey & Tomato Sauce

Servings: 4

Cooking Time: 30 Minutes

Ingredients:

- 2 tbsp canola oil
- 1 lb ground turkey
- 1 egg
- ¼ cup bread crumbs
- 2 cloves garlic, minced
- 1 tsp dried oregano
- 1 tsp cumin
- 1 tsp red pepper flakes
- Salt and pepper to taste
- 3 cups tomato sauce
- 8 oz rigatoni
- 2 tbsp grated Grana Padano

Directions:

1. In a bowl, combine turkey, crumbs, cumin, garlic, and egg. Season with oregano, salt, red pepper flakes, and pepper. Form the mixture into meatballs. Warm the oil on Sauté in your Instant Pot. Cook the meatballs for 3-4 minutes until browned on all sides; set aside.
2. Add rigatoni to the cooker and pour the tomato sauce over. Cover with water. Stir well. Throw in the meatballs. Seal the lid and cook for 4 minutes on High Pressure. Release the pressure quickly. Serve topped with cheese.

Desserts & Drinks

Desserts & Drinks

Lemon Cheesecake

Servings: 6

Cooking Time: 30 Minutes

Ingredients:

- Crust
- 20 vanilla wafers
- 1½ tablespoons almond slices, toasted
- 3 tablespoons melted butter
- Cheesecake Filling
- 12 ounces cream cheese, cubed and room temperature
- 2 tablespoons sour cream, room temperature
- ½ cup sugar
- 2 large eggs, room temperature
- Zest of 2 lemons, grated
- 1 tablespoon fresh lemon juice
- 1 teaspoon vanilla extract
- 2 cups water

Directions:

1. For Crust: Grease a 7" springform pan and set aside.
2. Add vanilla wafers and almonds to a food processor. Pulse to combine. Add in melted butter and pulse to blend. Transfer crumb mixture to springform pan and press down along the bottom and about ⅓ of the way up the sides of the pan. Place a square of aluminum foil along the outside of the bottom of the pan and crimp up around the edges.
3. For Cheesecake Filling: With a hand blender or food processor, cream together cream cheese, sour cream, and sugar. Pulse until smooth. Slowly add eggs, lemon zest, lemon juice, and vanilla extract. Pulse for another 10 seconds. Scrape the bowl and pulse until batter is smooth.
4. Transfer the batter into springform pan.
5. Pour the water into the Instant Pot. Insert the trivet. Set the springform pan on the trivet. Lock lid.
6. Press the Manual button and adjust time to 30 minutes. When the timer beeps, quick-release pressure until float valve drops and then unlock lid. Lift pan out of Instant Pot. Let cool at room temperature for 10 minutes.
7. The cheesecake will be a little jiggly in the center. Refrigerate for a minimum of 2 hours to allow it to set. Release side pan and serve.

Root Beer Float Cupcakes

Servings: 12

Cooking Time: 18 Minutes

Ingredients:

- Cupcakes
- ½ box moist vanilla cake mix
- 6 ounces (½ can) root beer
- 2 cups water
- Vanilla Buttercream
- 1 cup confectioners' sugar
- ⅓ cup unsalted butter, softened
- ½ teaspoon vanilla extract
- 1 tablespoon whole milk

Directions:

1. Grease twelve silicone cupcake liners.
2. In a medium bowl, combine cake mix and root beer. Spoon mixture into cupcake liners.
3. Add water to the Instant Pot and insert steam rack. Place six cupcake liners on steam rack. Lock lid.
4. Press the Manual or Pressure Cook button and adjust time to 9 minutes. When timer beeps, quick-release pressure until float valve drops. Unlock lid. Transfer cupcakes to a cooling rack. Repeat cooking process with remaining six cupcake liners.
5. To make buttercream, cream together vanilla buttercream ingredients in a medium mixing bowl. If buttercream is too loose, add a little more confectioners' sugar. If buttercream is too thick, add a little more milk.
6. Let cupcakes cool for at least 30 minutes until they reach room temperature, then spread buttercream on cooled cupcakes. Serve.

Spiced Red Wine–poached Pears

Servings: 4

Cooking Time: 13 Minutes

Ingredients:

- 4 ripe but still firm pears
- 2 tablespoons fresh lemon juice
- 4 cups dry red wine
- ½ cup freshly squeezed orange juice
- 2 teaspoons grated orange zest
- ¼ cup sugar
- 1 cinnamon stick
- ½ teaspoon ground cloves
- ½ teaspoon ground ginger
- 1 sprig fresh mint

Directions:

1. Rinse and peel the pears leaving the stem. Using a corer or melon baller, remove the cores from underneath without going through the top so you can maintain the stem. Brush the pears inside and out with the lemon juice.
2. Combine the wine, orange juice, orange zest, sugar, cinnamon stick, cloves, and ginger in Instant Pot. Press the Sauté button and then hit the Adjust button to change the temperature to More. Bring to a slow boil in about 3–5 minutes; stir to blend and dissolve the sugar. Carefully place the pears in liquid. Press Adjust button to change temperature to Less and simmer unlidded for 5 additional minutes. Lock lid.
3. Press Manual button and adjust time to 3 minutes. Use the Pressure button to set the pressure to Low. When the timer beeps, quick-release pressure until float valve drops and then unlock lid.
4. Use a slotted spoon to transfer the pears to a serving platter. Garnish with mint sprig.

Banana Bread Pudding

Servings: 4

Cooking Time: 20 Minutes

Ingredients:

- 4 cups cubed French bread, dried out overnight
- 2 small bananas, peeled and sliced
- ¼ cup granulated sugar
- 2 cups whole milk
- 3 large eggs
- ⅛ teaspoon salt
- 3 tablespoons unsalted butter, cut into 4 pats
- 1 ½ cups water

Directions:

1. Grease a 7-cup glass baking dish. Add bread, then banana slices. Sprinkle sugar evenly over bananas. Set aside.
2. In a small bowl, whisk together milk, eggs, and salt. Pour over ingredients in glass baking dish and place butter pats on top.
3. Add water to the Instant Pot and insert steam rack. Place glass baking dish on top of steam rack. Lock lid.
4. Press the Manual or Pressure Cook button and adjust time to 20 minutes. When timer beeps, quick-release pressure until float valve drops. Unlock lid.
5. Remove glass bowl from pot. Transfer to a cooling rack for 30 minutes until set. Serve.

Lemon-apricot Compote

Servings: 6

Cooking Time: 20 Minutes

Ingredients:

- 2 lb fresh apricots, sliced
- 1 lb sugar
- 2 tbsp lemon zest
- 1 tsp ground nutmeg
- 10 cups water

Directions:

1. Add apricots, sugar, water, nutmeg, and lemon zest. Cook, stirring occasionally until half of the water evaporates, on Sauté. Press Cancel and transfer the apricots and the remaining liquid into glass jars. Let cool. Refrigerate.

Rice Pudding

Servings:4

Cooking Time: 25 Minutes

Ingredients:

- 1 cup Arborio rice
- 1 ½ cups water
- 1 tablespoon vanilla extract
- 1 cinnamon stick
- 1 tablespoon unsalted butter
- 1 cup golden raisins
- ¼ cup granulated sugar
- ½ cup heavy cream

Directions:

1. Add rice, water, vanilla, cinnamon stick, and butter to the Instant Pot. Lock lid.
2. Press the Manual or Pressure Cook button and adjust time to 20 minutes. When timer beeps, let pressure release naturally for 10 minutes. Quick-release any additional pressure until float valve drops. Press the Cancel button. Unlock lid.
3. Remove cinnamon stick and discard. Stir in raisins, sugar, and heavy cream.
4. Press the Sauté button on the Instant Pot, press Adjust button to change temperature to Less, and simmer unlidded 5 minutes. Serve warm.

Pearberry Crisp

Servings:4

Cooking Time: 8 Minutes

Ingredients:

- Pearberry Filling
- 6 medium pears, peeled, cored, and diced
- 1 cup thawed frozen mixed berries
- ¼ cup water
- 1 tablespoon fresh lemon juice
- 2 tablespoons pure maple syrup
- 1 teaspoon ground cinnamon
- ¼ teaspoon ground nutmeg
- Pinch of salt
- Topping
- 4 tablespoons melted butter

- 1 cup old-fashioned oats
- ⅛ cup all-purpose flour
- ¼ cup chopped almonds
- ¼ cup packed light brown sugar
- ¼ teaspoon sea salt

Directions:

1. For Pearberry Filling: Place Pearberry Filling ingredients in Instant Pot. Stir to distribute ingredients.
2. For Topping: Mix Topping ingredients together in a small bowl. Spoon drops of topping over the filling. Lock lid.
3. Press the Manual button and adjust time to 8 minutes. When the timer beeps, let pressure release naturally until float valve drops and then unlock lid. Spoon into bowls and enjoy.

Cinnamon Applesauce

Servings:8

Cooking Time: 8 Minutes

Ingredients:

- 3 pounds apples (any variety), cored and chopped
- 1 teaspoon ground cinnamon
- ½ teaspoon ground allspice
- ½ cup granulated sugar
- ⅛ teaspoon salt
- ½ cup freshly squeezed orange juice
- ⅓ cup water

Directions:

1. Place all ingredients in the Instant Pot.
2. Press the Manual or Pressure Cook button and adjust time to 8 minutes. When timer beeps, quick-release pressure until float valve drops. Unlock lid.
3. Use an immersion blender to blend ingredients in pot until desired consistency is reached. Serve warm or cold.

Plum & Almond Dessert

Servings: 6

Cooking Time: 1 Hour 50 Minutes

Ingredients:

- 6 lb sweet ripe plums, pits removed and halved
- 2 cups white sugar
- 1 cup almond flakes

Directions:

1. Drizzle the plums with sugar. Toss to coat. Let it stand for about 1 hour to allow plums to soak up the sugar. Transfer the plum mixture to the Instant Pot and pour 1 cup of water. Seal the lid and cook on High Pressure for 30 minutes. Allow the Pressure to release naturally for 10 minutes. Serve topped with almond flakes.

Stuffed "baked" Apples

Servings:4

Cooking Time: 5 Minutes

Ingredients:

- ½ cup fresh orange juice
- ½ teaspoon orange zest
- ¼ cup packed light brown sugar
- ¼ cup golden raisins
- ¼ cup chopped pecans
- ¼ cup quick-cooking oats
- ½ teaspoon ground cinnamon
- 4 cooking apples
- 4 tablespoons butter, divided
- 1 cup water

Directions:

1. In a small bowl, mix together orange juice, orange zest, brown sugar, raisins, pecans, oats, and cinnamon. Set aside.
2. Rinse and dry the apples. Cut off the top fourth of each apple. Peel the cut portion of the apple. Dice it and then stir into the oat mixture. Hollow out and core the apples by cutting to, but not through, the apple bottoms.
3. Place each apple on a piece of aluminum foil that

is large enough to wrap the apple completely. Fill the apple centers with the oat mixture. Top each with 1 tablespoon butter. Wrap the foil around each apple, folding the foil over at the top and then pinching it firmly together.

4. Pour the water into Instant Pot. Set in trivet. Place the apple packets on the rack. Lock lid.
5. Press the Manual button and adjust time to 5 minutes. When timer beeps, let pressure release naturally for 10 minutes. Quick-release any additional pressure until float valve drops and then unlock lid.
6. Carefully unwrap apples and transfer to serving plates.

Stuffed Apples

Servings:4

Cooking Time: 10 Minutes

Ingredients:

- 4 Granny Smith apples
- 5 tablespoons unsalted butter, softened
- 2 teaspoons ground cinnamon
- ¼ cup packed light brown sugar
- ¼ teaspoon vanilla extract
- ¼ cup chopped walnuts
- ⅛ teaspoon salt
- 2 cups water

Directions:

1. Core apples, leaving some skin on bottom of hole to hold filling in place. Using a paring knife, remove just a little more of the apple center for a bigger area to fill.
2. In a medium bowl, combine butter, cinnamon, brown sugar, vanilla, walnuts, and salt. Stuff apples with this mixture. Place apples in a 7-cup baking dish.
3. Add water to the Instant Pot and insert steam rack. Place baking dish on steam rack.
4. Press the Manual or Pressure Cook button and adjust time to 10 minutes. When timer beeps, quick-release pressure until float valve drops. Unlock lid.
5. Allow apples to cool in pot 20 minutes. Serve warm.

Honey Homemade Almond Milk

Servings: 4

Cooking Time: 15 Minutes

Ingredients:

- 1 cup raw almonds, peeled
- 2 dried apricots, chopped
- 2 tbsp honey
- 1 vanilla bean
- ½ tsp almond extract

Directions:

1. In the Instant Pot, mix a cup of water with almonds and apricots. Seal the lid and cook for 1 minute on High. Release the pressure quickly. The almonds should be soft and plump, and the water should be brown and murky. Use a strainer to drain almonds and apricots. Rinse with cold water. To a blender, add the rinsed almonds and apricots, almond extract, vanilla bean, honey, and 4 cups water. Blend for 2 minutes until well combined and frothy. Line a cheesecloth to the strainer. Place the strainer over a bowl and strain the milk. Use a wooden spoon to press milk through the cheesecloth and get rid of solids. Place almond milk in an airtight container and refrigerate.

Yogurt Cheesecake With Cranberries

Servings: 6

Cooking Time: 45 Minutes + Chilling Time

Ingredients:

- 2 lb Greek yogurt
- 2 cups sugar
- 4 eggs
- 2 tsp lemon zest
- 1 tsp lemon extract
- 1 cheesecake crust
- For topping:
- 7 oz dried cranberries
- 2 tbsp cranberry jam
- 2 tsp lemon zest
- 1 tsp vanilla sugar
- 1 tsp cranberry extract
- ¾ cup lukewarm water

Directions:

1. In a bowl, combine yogurt, sugar, eggs, lemon zest, and lemon extract. With a mixer, beat well until well-combined. Place the crust in a greased cake pan and pour in the filling. Flatten the surface with a spatula. Leave in the fridge for 30 minutes. Combine cranberries, jam, lemon zest, vanilla sugar, cranberry extract, and water in the pot. Simmer for 15 minutes on Sauté. Remove and wipe the pot clean. Fill in 1 cup water and insert a trivet. Set the pan on top of the trivet and pour cranberry topping. Seal the lid and cook for 20 minutes on High Pressure. Do a quick release. Run a sharp knife around the edge of the cheesecake. Refrigerate. Serve and enjoy!

Creme Caramel With Whipped Cream

Servings: 4

Cooking Time: 30 Minutes + Cooling Time

Ingredients:

- ½ cup granulated sugar
- 4 tbsp caramel syrup
- 3 eggs
- ½ tsp vanilla extract
- ½ tbsp milk
- 5 oz whipping cream

Directions:

1. Combine milk, whipping cream, and vanilla extract in your Instant Pot. Press Sauté, and cook for 5 minutes, or until small bubbles form. Set aside. Using an electric mixer, whisk the eggs and sugar. Gradually add the cream mixture and whisk until well combined. Divide the caramel syrup between 4 ramekins. Fill with egg mixture and place them on the trivet. Pour in 1 cup water. Seal the lid and cook for 15 minutes on High Pressure. Do a quick release. Remove the ramekins and cool.

Best Tiramisu Cheesecake

Servings: 6

Cooking Time: 35 Minutes + Chilling Time

Ingredients:

- 1 ½ cups ladyfingers, crushed
- 1 tbsp Kahlua liquor
- 1 tbsp granulated espresso
- 1 tbsp butter, melted
- 16 oz cream cheese
- 8 oz mascarpone cheese
- 2 tbsp powdered sugar
- ½ cup white sugar
- 1 tbsp cocoa powder
- 1 tsp vanilla extract
- 2 eggs

Directions:

1. In a bowl beat the cream cheese, mascarpone, and white sugar. Gradually beat in the eggs, the powdered sugar, cocoa powder, and vanilla. Combine Kahlua liquor, espresso, butter, and ladyfingers, in another bowl. Press the ladyfinger crust at the bottom. Pour the filling on a greased cake pan. Cover the pan with aluminum foil. Pour 1 cup of water into your pressure cooker and lower a trivet. Place the pan inside and seal the lid. Select Manual and set to 25 minutes at High pressure. Release the pressure quickly. Allow cooling completely.

Catalan-style Crème Brûlée

Servings: 4

Cooking Time: 15 Minutes

Ingredients:

- 5 cups heavy cream
- 8 egg yolks
- 1 cup honey
- 4 tbsp sugar
- 1 vanilla extract
- 1 cup water

Directions:

1. In a bowl, combine heavy cream, egg yolks, va-nilla, and honey. Beat well with an electric mixer. Pour the mixture into 4 ramekins. Set aside. Pour water into the pot and insert the trivet. Lower the ramekins on top. Seal the lid and cook for 10 minutes on High Pressure. Do a quick pressure release. Remove the ramekins from the pot and add a tablespoon of sugar to each ramekin. Burn evenly with a culinary torch until brown. Chill well and serve.

Peachy Crisp

Servings:4

Cooking Time: 12 Minutes

Ingredients:

- 3 cups peeled, pitted, and diced peaches
- 4 tablespoons unsalted butter, melted
- ½ cup old-fashioned oats
- ⅛ cup all-purpose flour
- ¼ cup chopped almonds
- ⅓ cup granulated sugar
- ¼ teaspoon ground allspice
- ¼ teaspoon salt
- 1 cup water

Directions:

1. Place peaches in a 7-cup glass baking dish.
2. In a food processor, pulse together butter, oats, flour, almonds, sugar, allspice, and salt until butter is well distributed.
3. Preheat oven to broiler at 500°F.
4. Add water to the Instant Pot and insert steam rack. Lower glass baking dish onto steam rack. Lock lid.
5. Press the Manual or Pressure Cook button and adjust time to 8 minutes. When timer beeps, let pressure release naturally until float valve drops. Unlock lid.
6. Place dish under broiler 3–4 minutes until browned.
7. Serve warm or chilled.

Classic French Squash Tart

Servings: 6

Cooking Time: 35 Minutes

Ingredients:

- 15 oz mashed squash
- 6 fl oz milk
- ½ tsp cinnamon, ground
- ½ tsp nutmeg
- ½ tsp salt
- 3 large eggs
- ½ cup granulated sugar
- 1 pack pate brisee

Directions:

1. Place squash puree in a large bowl. Add milk, cinnamon, eggs, nutmeg, salt, and sugar. Whisk together until well incorporated. Grease a baking dish with oil. Gently place pate brisee creating the edges with hands. Pour the squash mixture over and flatten the surface with a spatula. Pour 1 cup of water into the pot and insert the trivet. Lay the baking dish on the trivet. Seal the lid, and cook for 25 minutes on High Pressure. Do a quick release. Transfer the pie to a serving platter. Refrigerate.

Festive Fruitcake

Servings:8

Cooking Time: 20 Minutes

Ingredients:

- 1 can crushed pineapple, including juice
- ½ cup raisins
- ½ cup dried unsweetened cherries
- ½ cup pitted and diced dates
- 1 cup pecan halves
- ½ cup chopped walnuts
- ½ cup unsweetened coconut flakes
- ½ cup sugar
- ¼ cup melted butter, cooled
- 2 teaspoons vanilla extract
- 2 tablespoons fresh orange juice
- 4 large eggs
- 1 cup all-purpose flour

- 2 teaspoons baking powder
- ¼ teaspoon salt
- ¼ teaspoon ground nutmeg
- 1 cup water

Directions:

1. In a medium bowl, combine all ingredients except water until well mixed. Grease a 6" cake pan. Press mixture into the pan.
2. Pour 1 cup water into the Instant Pot. Insert trivet. Lower 6" pan onto trivet. Lock lid.
3. Press the Manual button and adjust time to 20 minutes. When timer beeps, let pressure release naturally for 10 minutes. Quick-release any additional pressure until float valve drops and then unlock lid.
4. Remove fruitcake from Instant Pot and transfer to a cooling rack. Refrigerate covered overnight. Flip onto a cutting board, slice, and serve.

Spiced & Warming Mulled Wine

Servings: 6

Cooking Time: 20 Minutes

Ingredients:

- 3 cups red wine
- 2 tangerines, sliced
- ¼ cup honey
- 6 whole cloves
- 6 whole black peppercorns
- 2 cardamom pods
- 8 cinnamon sticks
- 1 tsp fresh ginger, grated
- 1 tsp ground cinnamon

Directions:

1. Add red wine, honey, cardamom, 2 cinnamon sticks, cloves, tangerine slices, ginger, and peppercorns. Seal the lid and cook for 5 minutes on High Pressure. Release pressure naturally for 10 minutes. Using a fine mesh strainer, strain the wine. Discard spices. Divide the warm wine into glasses. Garnish with cinnamon sticks to serve.

Chocolate Quinoa Bowl

Servings: 4

Cooking Time: 15 Minutes

Ingredients:

- 12 squares dark chocolate, shaved
- 2 tbsp cocoa powder
- 1 cup quinoa
- 2 tbsp maple syrup
- ½ tsp vanilla
- A pinch of salt
- 1 tbsp sliced almonds

Directions:

1. Put the quinoa, cocoa powder, maple syrup, vanilla, 2 ¼ cups water, and salt in your Instant Pot. Seal the lid, select Manual, and cook for a minute on High pressure. When ready, allow a natural release for 10 minutes and unlock the lid. Using a fork, fluff the quinoa. Top with almonds and dark chocolate and serve.

Homemade Walnut Layer Cake

Servings: 6

Cooking Time: 25 Minutes

Ingredients:

- ½ cup vanilla pudding powder
- 3 standard cake crusts
- ¼ cup granulated sugar
- 4 cups milk
- 10.5 oz chocolate chips
- ¼ cup walnuts, minced

Directions:

1. Combine vanilla powder, sugar, and milk in the inner pot. Cook until the pudding thickens, stirring constantly on Sauté. Remove from the steel pot. Place one crust into a springform pan. Pour half of the pudding and sprinkle with minced walnuts and chocolate chips. Cover with another crust and repeat the process. Finish with the final crust and wrap in foil.
2. Insert the trivet, pour in 1 cup of water, and place springform pan on top. Seal the lid and cook for 10 minutes on High Pressure. Do a quick release. Refrigerate.

Homemade Lemon Cheesecake

Servings: 6

Cooking Time: 1 Hour + Chilling Time

Ingredients:

- Crust:
- 4 oz graham crackers
- 1 tsp ground cinnamon
- 3 tbsp butter, melted
- Filling:
- 1 lb mascarpone cheese, softened
- ¾ cup sugar
- ¼ cup sour cream, at room temperature
- 2 eggs
- 1 tsp vanilla extract
- 1 tsp lemon zest
- 1 tbsp lemon juice
- A pinch of salt
- 1 cup strawberries, halved

Directions:

1. In a food processor, beat cinnamon and graham crackers to attain a texture almost same as sand; mix in melted butter. Press the crumbs into the bottom of a 7-inch springform pan in an even layer. In a stand mixer, beat sugar, mascarpone cheese, and sour cream for 3 minutes to combine well and have a fluffy and smooth mixture. Scrape the bowl's sides and add eggs, lemon zest, salt, lemon juice, and vanilla. Carry on to beat the mixture until you obtain a consistent color and all ingredients are completely combined. Pour filling over crust.
2. Into the inner pot, add 1 cup water and set in a trivet. Place the springform pan on the trivet. Seal the lid, press Cake, and cook for 40 minutes on High. Release the pressure quickly. Remove the cheesecake and let it cool. Garnish with strawberry halves on top. Use a paring knife to run along the edges between the pan and cheesecake to remove it and set it to a plate. Serve.

Cottage Cheesecake With Strawberries

Servings: 6

Cooking Time: 35 Minutes +cooling Time

Ingredients:

- 10 oz cream cheese
- ¼ cup sugar
- ½ cup cottage cheese
- 1 lemon, zested and juiced
- 2 eggs, cracked into a bowl
- 1 tsp lemon extract
- 3 tbsp sour cream
- 1 cup water
- 10 strawberries, halved to decorate

Directions:

1. Blend with an electric mixer, the cream cheese, quarter cup of sugar, cottage cheese, lemon zest, lemon juice, and lemon extract until a smooth consistency is formed. Adjust the sweet taste to liking with more sugar. Add the eggs. Fold in at low speed until incorporated. Spoon the mixture into a greased baking pan. Level the top with a spatula and cover with foil. Fit a trivet in the pot and pour in water. Place the cake pan on the trivet.
2. Seal the lid. Select Manual and cook for 15 minutes. Mix the sour cream and 1 tbsp of sugar. Set aside. Once the timer has gone off, do a natural pressure release for 10 minutes. Use a spatula to spread the sour cream mixture on the warm cake. Let cool. Top with strawberries.

Pumpkin Pudding With Apple Juice

Servings: 4

Cooking Time: 20 Minutes

Ingredients:

- 1 lb pumpkin, chopped
- 1 cup granulated sugar
- ½ cup cornstarch
- 4 cups apple juice
- 1 tsp cinnamon, ground
- 3-4 cloves

Directions:

1. In a bowl, combine sugar and apple juice until sugar dissolves completely. Pour the mixture into the pot and stir in cornstarch, cinnamon, cloves, and pumpkin. Seal the lid, and cook for 10 minutes on High Pressure. Do a quick release. Pour in the pudding into 4 serving bowls. Let cool at room temperature and refrigerate overnight.

Cherry & Chocolate Marble Cake

Servings: 6

Cooking Time: 45 Minutes

Ingredients:

- 1 cup flour
- 1 ½ tsp baking powder
- 1 tbsp powdered stevia
- ½ tsp salt
- 1 tsp cherry extract
- 3 tbsp butter, softened
- 3 eggs
- ¼ cup cocoa powder
- ¼ cup heavy cream

Directions:

1. Combine flour, baking powder, stevia, and salt in a bowl. Mix well to combine and add eggs, one at a time. Beat well with a dough hook attachment for one minute. Add heavy cream, butter, and cherry extract. Continue to beat for 3 more minutes. Divide the mixture in half and add cocoa powder in one-half of the mixture. Pour the light batter into a greased baking dish. Drizzle with cocoa dough to create a nice marble pattern. Pour in one cup of water and insert the trivet. Lower the baking dish on top. Seal the lid and cook for 20 minutes on High Pressure. Release the pressure naturally for 10 minutes.

Peanut Butter Custards

Servings:4

Cooking Time: 18 Minutes

Ingredients:

- 4 large egg yolks
- 2 tablespoons granulated sugar
- ⅛ teaspoon salt
- ¼ teaspoon vanilla extract
- 1 ½ cups heavy whipping cream
- ¾ cup peanut butter chips
- 2 cups water

Directions:

1. In a small bowl, whisk together egg yolks, sugar, salt, and vanilla. Set aside.
2. In a small saucepan over medium-low heat, heat cream to a low simmer, about 2 minutes. Whisk a spoonful of warm cream mixture into egg mixture to temper eggs. Then slowly add egg mixture back into saucepan with remaining cream.
3. Add peanut butter chips and continually stir on simmer until chips are melted, about 8–10 minutes. Remove from heat and evenly distribute mixture among four custard ramekins.
4. Add water to the Instant Pot and insert steam rack. Place steamer basket on steam rack. Place ramekins into basket. Lock lid.
5. Press the Manual or Pressure Cook button and adjust time to 6 minutes. When timer beeps, let pressure release naturally for 10 minutes. Quick-release any additional pressure until float valve drops. Unlock lid.
6. Transfer ramekins to a plate and refrigerate covered at least 2 hours or up to overnight. Serve chilled.

Amazing Fruity Cheesecake

Servings: 6

Cooking Time: 35 Minutes

Ingredients:

- 1 ½ cups graham cracker crust
- 1 cup raspberries
- 3 cups cream cheese
- 1 tbsp fresh orange juice
- 3 eggs
- ½ stick butter, melted
- ¾ cup sugar
- 1 tsp vanilla paste
- 1 tsp orange zest

Directions:

1. Insert the tray into the pressure cooker, and add 1 cup of water. Grease a springform. Mix in graham cracker crust with sugar and butter in a bowl. Press the mixture to form a crust at the bottom. Blend the raspberries and cream cheese with an electric mixer. Crack in the eggs and keep mixing until well combined. Mix in orange juice, vanilla paste, and orange zest. Pour this mixture into the pan, and cover the pan with aluminum foil. Lay the springform on the tray. Select Pressure Cook and cook for 20 minutes on High. Once the cooking is complete, do a quick pressure release. Refrigerate the cheesecake.

Quick Coconut Treat With Pears

Servings: 2

Cooking Time: 15 Minutes

Ingredients:

- ¼ cup flour
- 1 cup coconut milk
- 2 pears, peeled and diced
- ¼ cup shredded coconut

Directions:

1. Combine flour, milk, pears, and shredded coconut in your Pressure cooker. Seal the lid, select Pressure Cook and set the timer to 5 minutes at High pressure. When ready, do a quick pressure release. Divide the mixture between two bowls. Serve.

Measurement Conversions

BASIC KITCHEN CONVERSIONS & EQUIVALENT

DRY MEASUREMENTS CONVERSION CHART

3 TEASPOONS = 1 TABLESPOON = 1/16 CUP

6 TEASPOONS = 2 TABLESPOONS = 1/8 CUP

12 TEASPOONS = 4 TABLESPOONS = 1/4 CUP

24 TEASPOONS = 8 TABLESPOONS = 1/2 CUP

36 TEASPOONS = 12 TABLESPOONS = 3/4 CUP

48 TEASPOONS = 16 TABLESPOONS = 1 CUP

METRIC TO US COOKING CONVER SIONS

OVEN TEMPERATURE

120℃ = 250° F

160℃ = 320° F

180℃ = 350° F

205℃ = 400° F

220℃ = 425° F

OVEN TEMPERATURE

8 FLUID OUNCES = 1 CUP = 1/2 PINT = 1/4 QUART

16 FLUID OUNCES = 2 CUPS = 1 PINT = 1/2 QUART

32 FLUID OUNCES = 4 CUPS = 2 PINTS = 1 QUART = 1/4 GALLON

128 FLUID OUNCES = 16 CUPS = 8 PINTS = 4 QUARTS = 1 GALLON

BAKING IN GRAMS

1 CUP FLOUR = 140 GRAMS

1 CUP SUGAR = 150 GRAMS

1 CUP POWDERED SUGAR = 160 GRAMS

1 CUP HEAVY CREAM = 235 GRAMS

VOLUME

1 MILLILITER = 1/5 TEASPOON

5 ML = 1 TEASPOON

15 ML = 1 TABLESPOON

240 ML = 1 CUP OR 8 FLUID OUNCES

1 LITER = 34 FL. OUNCES

WEIGHT

1 GRAM = .035 OUNCES

100 GRAMS = 3.5 OUNCES

500 GRAMS = 1.1 POUNDS

1 KILOGRAM = 35 OUNCES

US TO METRIC COOKING CONVERSIONS

1/5 TSP = 1 ML

1 TSP = 5 ML

1 TBSP = 15 ML

1 FL OUNCE = 30 ML

1 CUP = 237 ML

1 PINT (2 CUPS) = 473 ML

1 QUART (4 CUPS) = .95 LITER

1 GALLON (16 CUPS) = 3.8 LITERS

1 OZ = 28 GRAMS

1 POUND = 454 GRAMS

BUTTER

1 CUP BUTTER = 2 STICKS = 8 OUNCES = 230 GRAMS = 8 TABLESPOONS

BUTTER

1 CUP = 8 FLUID OUNCES

1 CUP = 16 TABLESPOONS

1 CUP = 48 TEASPOONS

1 CUP = 1/2 PINT

1 CUP = 1/4 QUART

1 CUP = 1/16 GALLON

1 CUP = 240 ML

BAKING PAN CONVERSIONS

1 CUP ALL-PURPOSE FLOUR = 4.5 OZ

1 CUP ROLLED OATS = 3 OZ 1 LARGE EGG = 1.7 OZ

1 CUP BUTTER = 8 OZ

1 CUP MILK = 8 OZ

1 CUP HEAVY CREAM = 8.4 OZ

1 CUP GRANULATED SUGAR = 7.1 OZ

1 CUP PACKED BROWN SUGAR = 7.75 OZ

1 CUP VEGETABLE OIL = 7.7 OZ

1 CUP UNSIFTED POWDERED SUGAR = 4.4 OZ

BAKING PAN CONVERSIONS

9-INCH ROUND CAKE PAN = 12 CUPS

10-INCH TUBE PAN =16 CUPS

11-INCH BUNDT PAN = 12 CUPS

9-INCH SPRINGFORM PAN = 10 CUPS

9 X 5 INCH LOAF PAN = 8 CUPS

9-INCH SQUARE PAN = 8 CUPS

Dietary considerations when eating out

Research menus: Review dietary options and allergen information before eating out.

Portion control: Share dishes or ask take-out containers to indicate portion sizes.

Customize: Modify dishes to meet dietary needs.

Avoid Sugar: Limit sugary drinks and desserts.

Eat mindfully: Listen for hunger cues and eat slowly.

Hydrate: Drink water and avoid sugary drinks.

Avoid overeating: Watch for appetizers and side dishes.

Special Dietary Needs: Inform the server about allergies.

Ask questions: Be clear about ingredients and portion sizes.

Avoid fast food: Choose healthier restaurants.

Flexibility: Balance dietary goals with occasional indulgences.

Recipe

From the kicthen of . . . .

Serves . . . . Prep time . . . . Cook time . . . .

☐ Difficulty   ☐ Easy   ☐ Medium   ☐ Hard

Ingredient

. . . .

. . . .

. . . .

. . . .

. . . .

Directions

. . . .

. . . .

. . . .

. . . .

. . . .

RECIPES

DATE

RECIPES	Salads	Meats	Soups
SERVES	Grains	Seafood	Snack
PREP TIME	Breads	Vegetables	Breakfast
COOK TIME	Appetizers	Desserts	Lunch
FROM THE KITCHEN OF	Main Dishes	Beverages	Dinners

INGREDIENTS

DIRECTIONS

NOTES

SERVING ☆☆☆☆☆

DIFFICULTY ☆☆☆☆☆

OVERALL ☆☆☆☆☆

Appendix : Recipes Index

Made in the USA
Las Vegas, NV
28 December 2023

83655232R00063